'The anthology *Writers Under Siege* is essential reading for anyone who has ever been moved by the written word. The authors of these pieces have one thing in common. They have all been coerced into not writing.

This means that not only do they have powerful stories to tell, but that when, thanks very often to the work of organisations like PEN, they are eventually allowed to tell them, the result is spare, powerful writing, which jolts and challenges our prejudices and assumptions.

This is an inspiring and important book. Inspiring because by reading it we learn something new about the power of the written word and important because by writing it, those who have suffered are granted some redress for the brutality they've had to endure.

It's also important to realise that without PEN these extraordinary stories may never have seen the light of day. All too often PEN is the last recourse of those demanding that simple freedom which so many of us take for granted. To speak honestly and to be heard.' MICHAEL PALIN

'PEN acts as the voice and conscience of everyone who cares about literature. In telling their stories, the incredible writers in this collection uncover some of the world's darker corners. This extraordinary book shows us once again why literature matters.' ANTONIA FRASER

'This remarkable book should be a set text in every sixth form in the land, to spread the word that although man's inhumanity to man is boundless, so are the resources of strength and spirit which always challenge it. The truth is, we live under one sky, and so a sense of common destiny is the only hope in the perpetual fight against evil.' BEL MOONEY

'Engrossing. Reza Baraheni's piece is simply electric and others, such as Ken Saro-Wiwa's letters, are deeply moving. More than anything the colle
courage and a clarion call to
it really is – a basic human ri

D0377222

'I defy readers not to be profoundly moved by this splendid anthology. But I have no doubt they will also be stirred by the extraordinary courage of all these writers to triumph over injustice and cruelty. This book is an inspiration.'
RONALD HARWOOD

'These are extraordinary writers who take the reader to the very fault lines where freedom and oppression collide. From Turkey to China, from Russia to Iran, and beyond. Amid the evolving new world disorder these are vital and accessible insights into the issues we fail to address at our peril. Yet none of these writers preaches at us, all of them inform us through their exceptional qualities as story tellers. This is both a literary collection, and a political armament against those who turn a blind eye to human rights abuse.' JON SNOW

English PEN is the founding centre of an international association of writers. With 144 centres worldwide, PEN has three core aims: promoting literature, defending freedom of expression and developing a world community of readers and writers. The Writers in Prison Committee of English PEN sets up relationships between English writers and their imprisoned or persecuted colleagues around the world. These unique relationships, many of which endure over decades, exemplify the spirit of solidarity which underpins PEN's work.

LUCY POPESCU has worked with PEN's Writers in Prison Committee for fifteen years and writes a column for *Literary Review*.

CAROLE SEYMOUR-JONES, chair of the committee, is the biographer of Beatrice Webb and Vivienne Eliot and is now writing a book on Jean-Paul Sartre and Simone de Beauvoir.

WRITERS UNDER SIEGE

Voices of freedom from around the world

A **pen** ANTHOLOGY

Edited by

Lucy Popescu and Carole Seymour-Jones

NEW YORK UNIVERSITY PRESS
Washington Square, New York

First published in the United States of America in 2007 by
NEW YORK UNIVERSITY PRESS
Washington Square
New York, NY 10003
www.nyupress.org

LIBRARY OF CONGRESS CATALOGING-IN-PUBLICATION DATA
Writers under siege : voices of freedom from around the world :
a PEN anthology / edited by Lucy Popescu and Carole Seymour-
Jones ; with an introduction by Tom Stoppard.
    p. cm.
Includes bibliographical references and index.
ISBN-13: 978-0-8147-6742-9 (cloth : alk. paper)
ISBN-10: 0-8147-6742-7 (cloth : alk. paper)
ISBN-13: 978-0-8147-6743-6 (pbk. : alk. paper)
ISBN-10: 0-8147-6743-5 (pbk. : alk. paper)
1. Literature—Collections 2. Literature—Translations into
English. I. Popescu, Lucy. II. Seymour-Jones, Carole. III. PEN
(Organization)
  PN6014.W695   2007
    808.8'00511—dc22   2007014892

New York University Press books are printed on acid-free paper,
and their binding materials are chosen for strength and durability.

c 10 9 8 7 6 5 4 3 2 1
p 10 9 8 7 6 5 4 3 2 1

И тут-же подумаешь, что пройдут целые годы, а ты точно также пойдешь смотреть сквозь щели забора и увидишь тот-же вал, таких-же часовых и тот-же маленький краешек неба, не того неба, которое над острогом, а другого, далекого, вольного неба.

Ф. М. Достоевский, Записки из Мертвого Дома

… and then you would think that whole years would go by, and you would still come to look through the cracks in the fence and would see the same ramparts, the same sentries and the same little corner of sky, not the sky above the prison, but another sky, distant and free.

Fyodor Dostoevsky, *The House of the Dead*

… on se dit alors que des années entières s'écouleront et que l'on verra, par la même fente de palissade, toujours le même rempart, toujours les mêmes sentinelles et le même petit coin de ciel, non pas de celui qui se trouve au-dessus de la prison, mais d'un autre ciel, lointain et libre.

Fédor Dostoïevsky, *Souvenirs de la maison des morts*

…y de pronto piensas que pasarán años enteros y tú mirarás por las hendiduras del muro y sólo verás el baluarte, los mismos centinelas y ese mismo cachito de cielo, no de ese cielo de sobre la prisión, sino de otro cielo, lejano y libre.

Fedor Dostoievski, *Memorias de la casa muerta*

Contents

Sir Tom Stoppard   *Foreword*   xi

Carole Seymour-Jones   *Introduction*   xiv

Lucy Popescu   *A Note on Selections*   xxii

Harold Pinter   *'Death'*   xxvi

Ken Saro-Wiwa   *From his last television interview*   xxviii

Prison

Reza Baraheni, Iran / 'A Minor Mistake in Evin Prison'   3

Jiang Qisheng, China / 'A True Story of April Fool's Day',
translated by Ben Carrdus   10

Ali al-Dumaini, Saudi Arabia / Extract from *Time for Prison, Times
for Freedom,* translated by Judy Cumberbatch   17

Faraj Ahmad Bayrakdar, Syria / Extracts from *Mirrors of Absence,*
translated by Sinan Antoon   24

Asiye Güzel, Turkey / Extract from *Asiye's Story* translated by
Richard McKane   37

Augusto Ernesto Llosa Giraldo, Peru / 'Chiquitín' translated by
Amanda Hopkinson   45

Mamadali Makhmudov, Uzbekistan / Letter, translated by
Human Rights Watch   48

Yndamiro Restano, Cuba / 'Prison' translated by Mandy Garner;
Letter to PEN, translated by Maria Delgado   54

Faraj Sarkohi, Iran / Extract from *We Make Death Easy*, translated
by Nilou Mobasser   57

Angel Cuadra, Cuba / Poems translated by
Ruth Fainlight   64

Yury Bandazhevsky, Belarus / Extract from *The Philosophy of My Life*,
translated by Carole Seymour-Jones   68

Koigi wa Wamwere, Kenya / Extract from *Conscience on Trial*   76

Chris Abani, Nigeria / Poems   79

José Revueltas, Mexico / 'Letter to Arthur Miller', translated by
Amanda Hopkinson   87

Shi Tao, China / Poems, translated by Chip Rolley, Sarah Maguire
and Heather Inwood   93

Sihem Ben Sedrine, Tunisia / Letter, translated by
Cecilie Torjussen   96

Javier Tuanama Valera, Peru / 'Silent Impatience'   98

Grigory Pasko, Russia / Poems, translated by Richard McKane   101

Andrej Dynko, Belarus / 'Sacrificial therapy', translated by Ales'
Kudrycki   105

Thich Tue Sy, Vietnam / Poems, translated by Trevor Carolan and
Frederick Young   111

Hwang Dae-Kwon, South Korea / Letters   113

Khin Zaw Win, Burma / 'What I'm Doing'   123

Ali Reza Jabari, Iran / Letter   125

Flora Brovina, former Yugoslavia / 'The Freedom', translated by
Hans-Joachim Lankstch   129

Liu Jinsheng, China / Letter   131

Death

Ken Saro-Wiwa, Nigeria / Extract from his last work,
On the Death of Ken Saro-Wiwa   135

Thiagarajah Selvanithy, Sri Lanka / 'Undying Gardens',
translated by A. K. Ramanujan   141

Rakhim Esenov, Turkmenistan / 'The Death of the Poet', from
The Crowned Wanderer, translated by Rachel Segonds   143

Angel Cuadra, Cuba / 'A Man Dies, Cuba, 1964', translated by
Ruth Fainlight   149

Akbar Ganji, Iran / Extracts from *Dungeon of Ghosts*, translated by
Nilou Mobasser   150

Flora Brovina, former Yugoslavia / Poems, translated by
Hans-Joachim Lankstch   157

Harry Wu, China / Extract from *Thunderstorm in the Night*,
translated by Bernard F. Cleary   159

Chris Abani, Nigeria / 'Mango Chutney'   167

Exile

Gai Tho, India/Tibet / 'Once I Had a Home'   173

Raúl Rivero, Cuba / 'Family Picture in Havana', translated by
Diana Alvarez-Amell; 'After You, God', from *Pruebas de contacto*,
translated by Anna Kushner   175

Jean-Louis Ntadi, Congo-Brazzaville / *Cries of the Cricket*,
translated by Trevor Mostyn   182

Mansur Muhammad Ahmad Rajih, Yemen / Poems, translated by
Ren Powell and Mansur Rajih   193

Cheikh Kone, Ivory Coast / 'The Long Road'   199

Taslima Nasrin, Bangladesh / Extract from 'Mother', translated by
Taslima Nasrin and Warren Allen Smith   206

Chenjerai Hove, Zimbabwe / 'The Burdens of Creativity in Africa
– Reflections'   208

The Freedom to Write

Anna Politkovskaya, Russia / Essay, translated by Arch Tait · 217

Orhan Pamuk, Turkey / 'PEN Arthur Miller Freedom to Write
Memorial Lecture', translated by Maureen Freely 223

Aung San Suu Kyi, Burma / 'Freedom from Fear' 230

Paul Kamara, Sierra Leone / Extract from speech 237

Jiang Qisheng, China / 'Light a Myriad Candles ... An Open
Letter', translated by Ben Carrdus 242

Ma Thida, Burma / 'A Novel Response', translated by
Vicky Bowman 247

Hrant Dink, Turkey / Extract from speech 253

Hari Kunzru / 'Host Not Found' 259

Ken Saro-Wiwa, Nigeria / Letters 266

Acknowledgements 269

Permissions 270

Foreword

Sir Tom Stoppard

The founding purpose of PEN was, and remains, the promotion of translation, literature and literacy, but throughout its history – for eighty-five years – PEN has worked for the freedom of the writer. Here is an anthology to mark our eighty-fifth birthday and to celebrate PEN's work by giving a voice to persecuted writers by presenting their work in English to a new readership. Some of these writers are now free, which is something to celebrate, too; others are still in prison, and these we can help by publication and publicity – both are often effective levers for opening cell doors.

With centres in over one hundred countries, PEN has been supporting oppressed and marginalized individual writers since the early 1930s. The Writers in Prison Committee (WiPC) was formally set up in 1960 as a result of mounting concern about attempts to silence critical voices around the world. It works on behalf of all those who are detained or otherwise persecuted for their opinions expressed in writing and for writers who are under attack for their peaceful political activities or for the practice of their profession, provided that they did not use violence or advocate violence or racial hatred.

There are various ways to repress a writer or journalist who steps out of line. Increasingly writers, and freedom of expression, come under attack in those countries that have amended old laws or passed new ones in the name of fighting terrorism. Often trumped-up terrorist charges are used to convict those expressing opinions that those in power do not agree with.

It is worth noting that there has been a shift in recent years and with the exceptions of Burma, China, Cuba, Iran, Uzbekistan and Vietnam regimes are not always so keen to silence dissent through long-term imprisonment. Punishments range from hefty fines, banning, enforced exile, short detentions, torture and death threats to the ultimate form of censorship – murder. One of the most famous writers to have been executed in the last century is the Nigerian Ken Saro-Wiwa, and a powerful sense of the man and the writer endures through his words. Sadly just as this book was being completed, we learned of the murder of Anna Politkovskaya, the fearless Russian journalist, whose essay, written just a few weeks before her death, serves as a fitting example of the harrowing circumstances so many writers endure when practising their profession.

Today writers and journalists are attacked and even killed with impunity for speaking out against governments or about human rights abuses, and although the growth of the electronic media has allowed global communication, restrictive regimes, as in China and Tunisia, are using recent technology to target internet writers and imprison them. There are long-term detainees like Mamadali Makhmudov, in Uzbekistan, who has been serving a fourteen-year prison sentence since 1999. There are writers such as Ma Thida (Burma) and Rakhim Esenov (Turkmenistan) who have had their work censored or banned in their respective countries. Angel Cuadra (Cuba), Asiye Güzel (Turkey) and Chenjerai Hove (Zimbabwe) were forced to flee their countries and now live in exile.

The funds raised from this book will go towards English PEN's work for beleaguered writers around the world. This will ensure we can continue to lobby for their right to freedom of expression, campaign for an end to their persecution or imprisonment and offer support to their families when they come under attack. PEN attempts to highlight the situation of these courageous writers, publicizing their cases and raising their profile here and abroad. We adopt them as honorary members and send books and cards whenever possible. PEN makes no political distinctions between the hundreds of writers who are in prison or harassed, or between the governments who put them there. The concern is simply for men and women who are locked away, tortured or exiled because their writing is offensive or inconvenient to those that govern them.

Sir Tom Stoppard
October 2006

Introduction

This anthology bears witness to the power of the pen, and to an equally powerful longing for the right to use that pen without fear. Modern people, writes Orhan Pamuk, long for freedom of thought and expression 'as much as they long for bread and water'. That longing is so visceral, so deeply felt as an inalienable human right, that writers like Anna Politkovskaya and Ken Saro-Wiwa valued it over life itself. Martyrs for free speech, their iconic deaths demonstrate that in the twenty-first century freedom of expression is the just cause for which too many pay the ultimate price. Yet, as these vivid testimonies show, despite suffering and loss of liberty, the indomitable human spirit endures. I have been humbled by the courage of our contributors, whose incarceration reminds us that the struggle for writers' freedoms is one that every generation has to fight. It is a struggle that demands, more than ever, our hearts and minds, our commitment and our activism.

Although freedom of opinion and expression was recognized as a universal human right as long ago as 1948 in Article 19 of the Universal Declaration of Human Rights, it remains today under sustained, global assault. In 2006, a year which saw the increased polarization of East and West, International PEN documented over 1,000 writers, journalists and publishers in one hundred countries who were imprisoned and persecuted for exercising the right to write. Over the last two years, there have been over 400 uninvestigated cases of writers and journalists murdered with impunity. The need for the work of the Writers in Prison Committee of English PEN, the founding centre of the international writers' association, and the oldest human rights organization in the world, has never been more urgent. Internet giants Yahoo! and Google are co-operating with repressive governments to silence cyber-dissidence. In China, for example, Shi Tao and other cyber-dissidents are serving some of the longest sentences in the PEN casebook. In Europe, intimidated by fanaticism, governments waver in their defence of fundamental freedoms.

As the only writer-to-writer organization in the field of human rights, PEN is unique. From its foundation, the idea of writers' solidarity lay at the heart of English PEN. Few, perhaps, of the forty-one writers who attended the inaugural dinner in London in 1921 foresaw the future importance of writers defending other writers imprisoned for their views, but when John Galsworthy agreed to become English PEN's first president, he did so because 'Anything that makes for international understanding and peace is to the good.' From the beginning, PEN asked the question: 'If another writer is not free, how can any writer be free?'

With the rise of fascism, and the burning of books in Germany, the 1933 PEN Charter proclaimed that 'literature knows no frontiers' and declared for a free press. Members pledged themselves to oppose 'any form of suppression of freedom of expression in the country or community to which they belong'. As German intellectuals flocked to London to form the first PEN-in-Exile centre, the new president, H. G. Wells, proposed the establishment of a fund to support writers persecuted by their governments in any country.

In 1937 Arthur Koestler, in Spain on behalf of the *News Chronicle*, was arrested and condemned to death. A cable was sent to General Franco appealing for Koestler's release, signed by forty PEN members with the addition of E. M. Forster and Aldous Huxley. This first, vigorous campaign proved an outstanding success. Arriving in London, Koestler wrote to PEN to express his gratitude for:

> the unstinting help your organisation gave in obtaining my release. I am fully aware that it was no personal merit of my own, but in the deeper interests of freedom of expression of opinion, which is the life-blood of democracy and humanity, that this help is given.
>
> That a free public opinion should have thus proved so strong, is as much to me as my own personal liberty.

The Writers in Prison Committee (WiPC) was set up in 1960 at the suggestion of the Hungarian writer Paul Tabori to investigate the cases of writers imprisoned solely for the peaceful expression of their opinions, and to co-ordinate the actions of other PEN centres springing up abroad. Four years later Rosamond Lehmann (English PEN) became Chair of the Writers in Prison Committee, and Arthur Miller (US PEN) a member. At first the WiPC trod softly: appeals for clemency were confidential and diplomatic, and publicity was only used as a last resort.

In 1968 English PEN sent a member, Peter Elstob, to investigate the situation of the imprisoned playwright Wole Soyinka: the first PEN mission had been born. Further missions by Elstob followed, to Spain (on behalf of José Luis Méndez), South Korea (Kim Chi Hi) and South Africa (Breyton Breytenbach). Another innovation, and a tangible expression of solidarity, was the 'adoption' of imprisoned writers by national centres, who made them honorary members. WiPC members became 'minders' to individual prisoners, a process connecting writer to writer across national and cultural boundaries. Within International

PEN, writers found the space to assert their common humanity, and to act as *écrivains engagés*. The letters in *Writers Under Siege* demonstrate how this connection raises the status of imprisoned writers in the eyes of their colleagues and the prison authorities, as well as providing the psychological support of belonging to an international community of writers – the PEN family. 'Minders' also lobby governments, ambassadors and prison governors, send books to prisoners and support their families.

The Iranian writer Faraj Sarkohi wrote on his release:

> I have not been alone. Not in prison, nor on the torture bed, nor when they announced my death sentence. PEN was with me. I was rescued from prison and death. Where do I belong in exile? To nowhere except literature, the only concern that remained for me. To nowhere except PEN, the only family that remained for me.

Belatedly, PEN realized that in avoiding publicity it was neglecting its members' greatest strength, and turned to the media to mobilize opinion. Although the core work of campaigning for prisoners has greatly expanded, each case is carefully vetted in order to verify a writer's status before a campaign is launched. This strategy has made PEN a powerful, credible voice on behalf of oppressed writers, often resulting in release, shortened prison terms or the dropping of charges.

Sometimes, however, even the most passionate protest fails. This was the case with Ken Saro-Wiwa, whose last short story before his death appears in this anthology. Almost immediately after Saro-Wiwa's execution, Faraj Sarkohi was sentenced to death in Iran. His death sentence, allegedly for espionage and adultery but in reality for being the editor of the liberal journal *Adineh*, greatly alarmed Moris Farhi, then Chair of English PEN's

WiPC, and PEN members. 'We were quite distraught and feared that we would be facing another tragedy, so we decided to mount a weekly demonstration outside the Iranian embassy, protesting against his incarceration,' recalls Moris. PEN members gathered every Monday outside the embassy in London with banners and photographs, and were joined by Iranian exiles. When Faraj was eventually released and allowed to leave Iran for Germany, Moris met him at the German WiPC. 'We embraced and shed tears. Then I asked him, how did he recognize me? And he said that the guards in his prison would often tease him about the demonstrations in London and laugh at the fact that, according to the videos taken by Iranian Embassy personnel, the demos were led by a fat, white-haired old hippy. With that information, he said, he would recognize me anywhere.'

Antonia Fraser, Chair of our WiPC for three terms in the 1980s, recalls a similarly tense campaign for the Russian poet Irina Ratushinskaya. Demonstrations took place outside the Soviet Embassy; an English PEN petition was handed in and refused. This campaign, too, was crowned with victory when Irina was allowed to leave the USSR for the UK, where she gave birth to twins. 'It was a wonderful case from the PEN point of view,' recalls Antonia. 'I had read Irina's poems, translated by Richard McKane. PEN campaigns for all writers, but this case was particularly important. Irina is undoubtedly a great poet.'

Other successes have followed. Between 2005 and 2006 thirty-seven writers for whom PEN centres campaigned were released, including Yury Bandazhevsky, Ali-Reza Jabari, Ali Al-Domaini, Paul Kamara, U Sein Hla Oo and Jiang Weiping. Four petitions were organized, including one by English PEN on behalf of Mohammed Nasheed and Jennifer Latheef, pro-democracy activists in the Maldives charged with 'terrorism'. Our peaceful demonstration outside the Maldivian Embassy helped to raise awareness and bring about a pardon for Latheef from President Gayoom – renounced by her on the grounds that she could not be charged for something she had not done.

English PEN missions have expanded recently. In 2004 Ania Corless and Lucy Popescu went to Uzbekistan on behalf of Mamadali Makhmudov and Ruslan Sharipov. The following year Trevor Mostyn and I were delegates to Belarus, where Yury Bandazhevsky, the Chernobyl whistleblower, was held in prison in defiance of international condemnation. Since 2004 the main thrust of our missions, funded by the Foreign and Commonwealth Office, has been to provide a continuing English PEN presence monitoring, with other PEN centres (sixty-four of whom have WiPCs), the trials of freedom of expression cases in Turkey. This builds on the historic PEN mission to Turkey in 1985, when Harold Pinter and Arthur Miller went to investigate the plight of writers in prison, and Orhan Pamuk was their guide. Twenty years later, in December 2005, Pamuk himself faced trial for comments about the massacres of Armenians in the First World War. Over 400 British writers signed the English PEN petition protesting against Pamuk's arrest, and the charges were dropped on a technicality.

Over the last two years, WiPC members have continued to act as international observers at the trials of '301 cases' charged with 'insult' to Turkey. The English PEN delegates Maureen Freely, Alev Adil, Joan Smith, Jonathan Fryer and Richard McKane have attended the trials of Perihan Magden, Pinar Selek, Orhan Pamuk, Hrant Dink, Murat Belge, Fikret Baskaya, Ragip Zarakolu and others, witnessing the daily violence and intimidation by which these writers, journalists and publishers are harassed, but also hearing from them that the presence of PEN observers is effective in bringing about acquittal or the reduction of sentences. Elif Shafak, charged with 'insult' for comments made by a fictional character in her novel, *The Bastard of Istanbul*, was pardoned, but that is no cause for celebration. Sixty freedom of expression cases are set to come before the Turkish courts at the time of writing, demonstrating the urgent need for reform of the Turkish penal code.

Continuity and change have marked the development of English PEN, and its 'beating heart', the WiPC. In response to fresh challenges, we will work with the International WiPC on the themes of impunity and criminal defamation, and with the International Cities of Refuge Network (ICORN) to make increased provision within the UK for exiled writers. It is important for PEN to concentrate on what makes it unique, the writer-to-writer connection, and to collaborate with, but not duplicate, the work of other human rights organizations. In the area of cyber-dissent, as Hari Kunzru argues, human rights defenders need to move beyond the sphere of protest and lobbying to put anti-censorship tools into the hands of cyber-dissidents, rather than campaigning for their release after they have been imprisoned. As I write, only days after the murder of Anna Politkovskaya, widely interpreted as marking the extinction of liberal dissent in Russia, the threat to the uncensored voice is growing. This is not the time for those who deal in ideas to practise self-censorship; it is time to defend democracy.

The theme of the prisoner's journey has guided the arrangement of this anthology, which attempts to mirror the 'long journey', as the Burmese poet Khin Zaw Win describes it, from the horror of torture, suffering, illness and loss of liberty, to a mood of endurance, acceptance, even hope. As Siobhan Dowd, editor of an earlier PEN anthology, wrote, the prison experience can be 'a journey of moral transformation'. The prisoner's path divides, ending for some in death. Others face the challenge of exile in a strange land. The final section includes essays, articles and short stories from a range of contemporary commentators, including persecuted writers, on the freedom to write.

'Now more than ever it's vitally important to support those with the courage to speak in a fully human voice,' writes Margaret Atwood. 'The freedom to use that voice was hard-won, and must be defended whenever possible.'

Carole Seymour-Jones
Chair of the Writers in Prison Committee of English PEN[1]
October 2006

---

1 Acknowledgements: Josephine Pullein-Thompson, 'Standing Aside from Politics', *English PEN Broadsheet*, no. 19, Autumn 1985; Michael Scammell, 'Of International PEN', *English PEN Broadsheet*, no. 21, Autumn 1986

A Note on Selections

The Russian journalist Anna Politkovskaya was shot dead on 7 October 2006, and few doubt that her horrific murder is in retribution for her fearless reporting. She had been receiving threats since 1999 after writing articles claiming that the Russian armed forces had committed human rights abuses in Chechnya. Despite this she continued to write. Just before going to press the Turkish-Armenian writer and editor Hrant Dink was murdered in Istanbul on 19 January 2007. He too had been receiving death threats. The tragic deaths of Dink and Politkovskaya underlines the need to protect journalists like them, who write about human rights abuses in defiance of those who would silence them.

One of the aims of *Writers Under Siege* is to reflect not only the countries in which PEN works but also the wide range of writers PEN defends: poets, playwrights, essayists, novelists, academics, journalists, and increasingly cyber-dissidents; all these writing genres are included here. I have attempted to build on the work of a previous anthology, *This Prison Where I Live*, produced by International PEN, edited by Siobhan Dowd and published by Cassell in 1996. That is why there is nothing that predates the Mexican writer José Revueltas's letter to Arthur Miller in 1970 – Dowd covered the preceding period so thoroughly. Poems by Angel Cuadra (Cuba) and the extract from Harry Wu's book (China) refer to earlier times in prison but were not written until some years later. The majority of the contributions have not been published in book form before and some pieces, such as Hari Kunzru's essay on cyber-dissidence and Politkovskaya's disturbingly prescient article, were written exclusively for the anthology. Many of the translations, including those of Ali al-Dumaini (Saudi Arabia), Faraj Bayrakdar (Syria), Rakhim Esenov (Turkmenistan) and Augusto Ernesto Llosa Giraldo (Peru), were specifically commissioned by English PEN and generously funded by the Open Society Institute.

The book demonstrates the different ways a writer can be silenced and is structured accordingly, with sections on prison, death and exile. Examples of writing that actually landed the author in trouble are included, such as the Chinese writer Jiang Qisheng's open letter in remembrance of the Tiananmen Square massacre and two newspaper articles by the Iranian journalist Akbar Ganji. There is also an extract from Esenov's book *The Crowned Warrior*, banned in Turkmenistan. These sit alongside poems and prose written in prison and essays about freedom of expression by the Nobel Prize-winners Orhan Pamuk and Aung San Suu Kyi, as well as the late Dink and Politkovskaya.

There are several recurring themes in the collection. Over 150 years ago, Fyodor Dostoevsky wrote about 'another sky' in *The House of the Dead*, his book about life in a Siberian prison, based on his own experience. His motif is as relevant now as it was then and features in the work of a number of these contemporary writers.

Another theme is distance: many of the authors use their writing to create an emotional distance from the horrors they suffered. The Iranian writer Faraj Sarkohi once told me that every time a gun was held to his head, he recalled Beethoven's *Ode to Joy*, transporting him to another realm, and thereby giving him the necessary distance to ensure his survival. The extract from his novel is particularly telling in this respect. His main character attempts to describe his experience, but instead of relaying this at first hand Sarkohi invents a 'device' whereby his character is 'possessed by the spirit of the prisoner known as 612'. The prisoner of conscience reduced to a number. The dehumanizing effect of this is often brought up by writers who have been detained, and is particularly apparent in the work by asylum seekers, such as Cheikh Kone's account of his treatment in Australia after fleeing the Ivory Coast.

As well as distance, writing provides an escape – a way to cope with pain and torture. For some, writing becomes a means of survival, whether this is before, during or after the experience. Asiye Güzel, for example, gives a harrowing account of the rape she suffered, under interrogation in Turkey, while the Nigerian Chris Abani has produced some of the strongest and most heart-rending poems I have read about the experience of torture. You can read Güzel's full account in *Asiye's Story* and Abani's poems in *Kalakuta Republic*, both published by Saqi Books.

Of course, it is not always possible to write in prison, and many of the writers held in solitary confinement talk about befriending the various insects or rodents that inhabited their cells as an alternative to putting pen to paper and to help them remain sane. Ali al-Dumaini refers to the pet ant he named Wirda, while the Cuban Yndamiro Restano writes of the comfort offered by a spider who shares his space.

The pieces also cover a variety of moods. Occasionally there is humour – the Zimbabwean Chenjerai Hove's reflections have me laughing out loud, especially when he is there to deliver them in person. The personal warmth of the writers is often evident in their work – such as Bau's engaging letters from prison in South Korea, or Paul Kamara's speech on his persecution in Sierra Leone, which apparently left its Italian audience in tears.

Inevitably some writers PEN has helped in the past are omitted. Some are no longer in contact, others cannot be reached because they remain in prison or continue to live under a restrictive regime. It was wonderful to uncover Revueltas's letter to Arthur Miller. And quite coincidentally, the translator I approached, Amanda Hopkinson, had actually visited the writer when he was languishing in a Mexican prison in the early 1970s. It was also heartening to become reacquainted with work by writers PEN campaigned for ten or twenty years ago – such as the Kosovan poet Flora Brovina and the Kenyan writer and politician Koigi wa Wamwere, who are now able to write freely.

I remain in touch with a number of the writers contained in these pages. They are all survivors. On being released or finding a safe haven, some have fought for the rights of the compatriots they left behind, or continue to battle against repression. In the face of adversity others have forged new lives and learned to write in an unfamiliar language and alien landscape. As well as listening to horrific accounts of torture, I have also been privileged to share their laughter. I think the courage of them all shines through, paying testament to the strength of the human spirit. Their resilience and humour is inspirational. I hope you think so too.

PEN colleagues of course proved invaluable in producing this anthology – as well as everyone at the International headquarters, Anna Kushner and Larry Siems from American PEN were particularly supportive. Larry tracked down books in the United States and carted them across the world for me to read, and Anna was always ready with an address or the name of a contact who might be able to help, as well as sending me books and documents on request. Jaime Ramirez Garrido, of Mexican PEN, offered encouragement and imaginative advice. Elisabet Middelthon from Norwegian PEN, Moris Farhi, Richard McKane and Joan Smith from English PEN were always there to talk through things and offer their help.

Grateful thanks to them and to those translators who refused payment – donating their fee to PEN. You know who you are.

Hrant Dink, Anna Politkovskaya, Ken Saro-Wiwa and Thiagarajah Selvanithy: **Rest in Peace**

Lucy Popescu
October 2006

Death

(Births and Deaths Registration Act 1953)

Where was the dead body found?
Who found the dead body?
Was the dead body dead when found?
How was the dead body found?

Who was the dead body?

Who was the father or daughter or brother
Or uncle or sister or mother or son
Of the dead and abandoned body?

Was the body dead when abandoned?
Was the body abandoned?
By whom had it been abandoned?

Was the dead body naked or dressed for a journey?

What made you declare the dead body dead?
Did you declare the dead body dead?
How well did you know the dead body?
How did you know the dead body was dead?

Did you wash the dead body
Did you close both its eyes
Did you bury the body
Did you leave it abandoned
Did you kiss the dead body

Harold Pinter, 1997

From the last television interview conducted with Ken Saro-Wiwa before his imprisonment and execution

In this country [England], writers write to entertain, they raise questions of individual existence ... but for a Nigerian writer in my position you can't go into that. Literature has to be combative. You cannot have art for art's sake. This art must do something to transform the lives of a community, of a nation. And for that reason, literature has a different purpose altogether in that sort of society ...

What is of interest to me is that my art should be able to alter the lives of a large number of people, of a whole community, of the entire country, so that my literature has to be entirely different ...

The stories that I tell must have a different sort of purpose from the artist in the Western world ... and art, in that instance, becomes so meaningful both to the artist and to the consumers of that art, because you do not just depend on them to read your books, you even have to live a life that they can emulate.

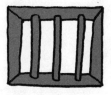

Section One

PRISON

A prison sentence is the beginning of a journey for every writer who finds him- or herself behind bars for exercising the right to write. Wherever the country, whatever the jail, the intention is the same: to silence the uncensored voice. The prisoner's journey may pass from despair to hope. Torture brings almost unimaginable suffering; illness, starvation, mental breakdown and acceptance are steps on the journey. The prisoner aches for that other sky, freedom. He may step out into the light, or the darkness of the grave. He may have to negotiate the pain of exile, the brutality of racism.

Reza Baraheni

Born in Tabriz, Iran, in 1935, Reza Baraheni is a poet and the author of several novels and short stories. He worked as professor of English at Tehran University and has also taught at universities in the USA and England. He was imprisoned during the time of the Shah in the 1970s and by the Islamic Republic of Iran in the early 1980s. He has served as PEN Canada's president and currently lives in Toronto.

The following recounts one memorable night Baraheni spent in Iran's notorious Evin Prison.

A minor mistake in Evin Prison

I was imprisoned for most of the autumn of 1981 and the first month of 1982. At first I was kept in the corridor of the Joint Committee, an old torture station from the Shah's regime that had been reactivated by the Islamic Republic of Iran. There were many women in the cells of the ward where I was being kept. So, the men remained in the corridor, with blindfolds covering their eyes, sleeping there, eating prison rations, and waiting. I stayed in these conditions for twenty-two days. Then I was moved to solitary confinement on the upper floor, where the blindfold was removed for the first time. After a month, I was blindfolded and taken by car to Evin prison. Here is the story of one particular night there.

As usual, I sat in the interrogation room, facing the wall. It

3

was late in the afternoon. My share of interrogation for the day had ended. I was waiting for them to blindfold me, take me out into the corridor, raise my arm onto the shoulder of someone ahead of me, and place someone else's hand on my shoulder. Then they would lead our column downstairs into the big lobby of the courthouse, and out into a waiting minibus, to be driven up the hill to our cells.

It was already dark when they came. They were working very fast. The blindfold was on my eyes in a minute. I could feel someone else as well as the guard. The two of us were taken into the corridor and our hands placed on other prisoners' shoulders. I didn't know how many of us were there. From downstairs, I could hear the bullying voices of the guards, scattered but loud.

Through the small cleft where the blindfold pressed against my nose and cheek, I could see wheelchairs passing by with swollen, bloody feet hanging from them. I could hear whispering, sighs and painful breathing. We were ordered to move, but the bustle and jostle around us was too heavy to allow us to go down the stairs. I kept gripping hard on the shoulder of the man ahead of me and felt the firm grip of the man behind me, and going down was utterly laborious. This night seemed different from other nights. Finally we were downstairs. It felt as if there were a million people whirling around my blindfolded eyes. The hand on my shoulder shook hysterically, and my own hand on the shoulder of the man ahead of me was no longer under my control. We stood there, as if there were only the three of us, jam-packed with all these other people jeering at us. Now, every whisper, every scream, every smell and movement had a thousand meanings.

Suddenly I noticed the shaking hand on my shoulder was no longer there. There were only the two of us, connected to each other by my arm, disconnected from the rest of the world behind the thick wall of the blindfold. I could no longer hold my arm straight and grip the shoulder of the unknown man ahead of me. It dropped by volition of its natural inertia. I stood alone and blind in a hostile world.

Had the audience forgotten the man on the stage? Was this the last scene? Where was my stick? Was the blinded Oedipus leaving the stage in utter ignominy? I don't know how long I stood there, but suddenly I heard the voice of authority: 'Put your hand on the shoulder of the person ahead of you and walk!' What a relief! What a moment of bliss! I would be in my cell in less than twenty minutes. At the end of the day's grilling, I felt I had convinced my interrogator that I hadn't done anything that would be considered treason. And now, in a few minutes, I could sum up in my mind the pros and cons of the situation and prepare myself for the next round of the interrogation. I raised my hand briskly and put it on the shoulder of the man ahead of me, and almost simultaneously felt the hand of the man behind me on my shoulder, and we set out, emerging into the open air.

The cold weather did not hurt at all. There must be stars up in the freezing sky, I thought. If only the blindfold were removed! We were ordered to walk, and walk we did, slowly and precariously, hunched up subhuman beings, each with the hope in mind of one day straightening his back and looking up at the sky with free, open eyes. But this was not normal! Where were the minibuses? We were walking on rough ground. There was silence, it was dark, and I sensed the dim streaks of something like flashlights, or meteorites, in the sky.

'Where are they taking us?'

I feel a strange pressure on my shoulder from the hand of the man behind me. But I cannot stop talking: 'Where! Where are they taking us?'

Others don't speak. I hear the barking of a dog in the distance and the coughing of someone nearby. And then the man from behind me says, 'Don't you know?'

'I've always been taken to my cell after interrogation. We never walked. They took us in the minibus.'

'We were in court. We're being taken to be shot.'

'What!'

'You mean you weren't in the court with us?'

'No! I wasn't in any court.'

'I must have put my hand on the shoulder of the wrong man in the confusion. You must have done the same. There were too many people there.'

I don't know what to do. My whole mind is a vegetable. I try to call out to the guards. I have no voice. Cold sweat is running down all over me.

'Have they marked the soles of your feet?'

'What!'

'Have they marked the soles of your feet?

'No!'

'They've marked the soles of our feet with a marker that we're to be shot.'

'I've no such things on the soles of my feet.'

'What are you waiting for! Just shout and tell them.'

This time I shouted at the top of my voice: 'Guard! Brother Passdar! There's been a mistake! I wasn't in court! Come and look at the soles of my feet!'

'Shut up, you bastard infidel!' It is the voice of the Passdar all right.

The man from behind says, 'Keep screaming. Tell them to come and look at the soles of your feet.'

I scream. I don't know what I am saying, but I know I am fighting for my life. My hand is still on the shoulder of the man walking ahead of me.

'Take off your shoes and scream. Tell them about the soles.' The man from behind me is the only one who speaks. He doesn't think of himself at all. What kind of a human being is he?

'Come and look at the soles of my feet!' I scream, trying to take off my shoe, but it is impossible with my hand on someone's shoulder and someone else's hand on my shoulder. Anyway, how can I show the soles of my feet to anyone in the dark? 'It's impossible! It's impossible!' I whisper.

'Do what you can to stay alive. We've lost our lives, perhaps for a reason. But why should you lose yours?'

I scream, thinking that it would be an honour to die beside this man.

'You godless bastard! You think you can save your skin by screaming. I'll show you when I shoot you myself in ten minutes!'

'But come and look at the soles of my feet. See for yourself. I wasn't in court. I was being interrogated by Hadji-Agha Hosseini the whole day. The interrogation isn't finished yet! Why don't you believe me?'

'Don't tire! Scream!' the man whispers.

And I scream, no matter what. And the guard swears. And we reach the final destination.

We are all panting. There are many flashlights. There are many people, talking in whispers. Some of them must be the firing squad. Others are there too, perhaps as spectators, to see what would happen to them if they didn't recant and betray their friends. They have to see the face of death to make up their mind.

'Brother Passdar, please, come and take a look at the soles of my feet. You will see that I was not condemned to death.'

'Shut up!' A voice louder than anything before reverberates in the silence.

Someone says, 'I want you to remove the blindfold before shooting me. I want to see the night of Tehran once more before I die.'

'Shut up! That's all.'

There are two men crying in the distance. One of them keeps saying, 'God, is this the end of my life?'

Someone comes towards us and we are told to walk, and then we are separated. As soon as I am alone, I take off my shoes and stand barefoot, waiting. Someone asks: 'Eight or nine?'

Someone answers: 'Nine.'

'Take off my blindfold!' It is the voice of the man who wants to see the night of Tehran.

Someone says, 'Remove his blindfold.' I don't speak any more. Barefoot, I wait.

Then I sense the hurried streaking of the flashlights. Perhaps it is not the fear of death that is so horrible. It is the waiting itself, for death. The flashlight moves closer, spreading its light on the ground. The man is taking off his shoes. Then someone tells him to put on his shoes. I hear him replace his shoes.

Then it is my turn. I tell the Passdar bending before me to examine the soles of my feet to see for himself that there has been a mistake. But he doesn't let me go on. He calls out, 'Hassan, come and take this man to the courthouse and have them mark the soles of his feet.'

I put my shoes back on. Someone grabs my hand and pulls me away. He keeps me blindfolded, and starts to run, making me run blindly downhill. He doesn't ask questions, but I keep telling him that I am innocent, and I keep thinking that running like this might even result in an earlier death, before the one by firing squad.

Scribbling something on the sole of my foot equals death. How dangerous writing can be! The man pulling me over the craggy path doesn't say anything. How long it takes to get there. I no longer say anything.

When we finally stop and enter the courthouse, my head goes dizzy and I am about to throw up. What is this? They are having soup. I remember having had soup once when we were delayed in the interrogation room. I also remember the jokes about the soup, said to have been made by the head chef of the Hilton Hotel, who had been arrested.

I begin to shout at the top of my voice that I hadn't been to court and was innocent. Hassan calls out to someone else, asking him to come and mark my foot. The man comes over and the first thing he asks me for is my name. I hear him going through something like a file. 'Hold him right here,' he says and departs. A minute later, there is chaos in the lobby of the courthouse. They have ordered everyone to take off their shoes. Then I hear a clapping of hands. No, it is a slap on someone's face. It feels as if someone is being beaten up. There are people running, and suddenly someone is pushed up before my very nose. 'Let go of him! Take this one up!' The grip on my wrist loosens.

I would very much like to see the face of the man who is going to be taken up the craggy path. He is breathing hard. He smells of the soup he has just eaten. We stand only for a minute, facing each other in the dark, with the smell from his mouth reaching my nostrils. Then they depart. I stand there. A few minutes later, someone takes my hand and leads me to a corner and tells me to sit down. Through the gap underneath the blindfold I see a half-eaten bowl of soup with an aluminium spoon in it. I can hear others eating. The man stands by me for some time, then he says, 'Eat!' I take the spoon, and when I am about to raise it to my mouth, I hear the shots, loud and clear. I put the spoon back in the bowl.

Jiang Qisheng

Jiang Qisheng was born in China in 1948. A pro-democracy activist, Qisheng was arrested on 18 May 1999 and charged with 'propagating and instigating subversion' for writing and distributing an open letter to commemorate the tenth anniversary of the 4 June crackdown in Tiananmen Square. Qisheng also called on the Chinese people to light candles in memory of those killed in the 1989 suppression of the pro-democracy movement. The courts deliberated over the case until 27 December 2000, when Qisheng was finally sentenced to four years in prison.

Qisheng has frequently published articles in the overseas Chinese magazine *Beijing Spring*. He has reportedly been active in the dissident community in Beijing since 1989, and has been detained on several other occasions for his dissident activities.

The following is an extract from his prison diary, 1999–2003

A true story of April Fool's Day

The 1st of April 2001 was a Sunday and my third day in prison following my transfer from the detention centre. There was glorious sunshine outside; inside the room the light from the window was barely any brighter than usual. As was the way with the detention centre, there were only two meals here on a Sunday – there was no breakfast – and therefore there was more time for cleaning. According to the group leader, the cleaning had to be done to the highest standards that day. When the brigade leader came into the room and ran his finger across any surface, there couldn't be even the smallest speck of dirt anywhere. I was responsible for scrubbing the crockery cupboards. I went over one with a damp cloth first, then a dry one, and then with just my hand, repeating the same process over and over again on all of the cupboards.

Spending an entire day cleaning was the only time we could ever move of our own volition, the only time we could physically move our bodies without being ordered or having to ask permission. And so slowly, carefully, and without complaining we worked in calm and restful silence.

As far as life in the prison was concerned, once the cleaning was finished on a Sunday all of the rules and regulations were the same as in the detention centre before. First, there was shouting with all of your might, 'Reporting present and correct!', followed by running four circuits of the yard, then running on the spot. The only minor difference was that the exercise drill was slightly shorter on this day.

After exercise, the group leader ordered us to fetch the wooden boards with the 'ten forbiddens' written on them, and then had everyone sit and 'study' together. As usual I didn't read out loud with the person leading the recitations. I must have looked like an illiterate fool who was actually taking in the ten forbiddens.

On the evening of 30 March I'd told the group leader I was innocent, that there was no way I could be reformed, and naturally I wouldn't therefore be memorizing the 'Standards for the Reform of Criminal Behaviour'. The group leader wasn't put out in the slightest, saying only that all political criminals were like that. The following afternoon, the group was being taught the prison song, called 'Shout out one-two-one, Keep your head up high!' The group leader said I didn't have to sing. I said that when they didn't shout out one-two-one, their heads always dropped. And why should I lower my head? There's the old saying, 'The guilty lower their heads in shame' – I'm innocent, so why should I lower my head? The group leader told me to stop talking. You're you, they're them, he said, and they have to learn the standards and sing the song.

Soon after, the duty-man told all of the groups that visitors from a bank were due to be shown around. I didn't understand. What were these white-collar workers from the upper echelons of society doing coming here to see society's lowest echelons? I later realized that these young men and women were being shown the inside of a prison as a warning, a reminder to think again if they ever thought of doing something impetuous with all of that money. As one of the people being observed, I don't think I was quite what the leaders at the bank intended their staff to see. But the other prisoners were as concerned about 'face' as ever, and projected all of the 'civilization' and 'humanity' they could by cleaning the prison.

It was almost ten o'clock on 1 April when we heard the sound of the electric steel gates being opened, and a line of some seventy immaculately dressed bank personnel filed into the prison. Under the careful planning and detailed organization of the prison, no one saw any electric cattle prods, and no one heard any screams. Instead, they all stepped onto a cleanly swept path where the first thing they saw was a building hung with the signs 'Library' and 'Psychological Counselling Room', while in the corner of one of the rooms inside was a 34-inch colour television. They continued on and saw the bright and clean toilets and washrooms; they went through the dormitories, signposted from 'Group One' through to 'Group Eight' and all identically arranged around study areas where prisoners in uniform sat pressed together in silence, concentrating on their 'studies'. No one looked up or around; no one so much as whispered.

This whole series of eight sweatshops had been immaculately swept and 'converted' into prison dormitories. All of the workbenches and machines had been stowed away. Even the sharpest eyesight would have missed the minuscule clues that showed this was in fact a workshop. Every single mattress on the prisoners' beds was exactly the same thickness and they all had exactly the same sheets; and the deep blue duvets were all arranged and placed in exactly the same position at the foot of the bed. There was something even more military than the military about the scene.

But the good bank workers would never have noticed such details; and nor could they have possibly known that stuffed into the space under each of the beds was the bedding that the prisoners actually used. Sadly, those threadbare and faded bedrolls could not speak; sadly, the prisoners in those rooms who knew the truth of it all were too terrified to speak. And so it was that these young white-collar merchants, these handsome young men and beautiful young women, were publicly duped on April Fool's Day.

As with the bank workers, every single prisoner was also duped when he first arrived in the prison; the difference was that by the evening of the same day, the prisoner would know he had been duped. For example, I was fooled on the morning of 30 March, but by eleven o'clock that evening, I knew someone had played a trick on me. I remember walking into the prison that morning, and feeling pleasantly surprised by the neat rows of iron beds and the duvets and bedclothes. I thought at the time that if the prison uniforms and shoes were issued, then mattresses and bedclothes were obviously issued too.

On 30 March at nine o'clock (bedtime in the detention centre), I was suddenly overcome with tiredness and doubted I'd be able to stay awake until eleven o'clock. Just when I thought I might open out my deep blue duvet and sleep soundly in my very own bed, a completely unexpected scene exploded into action before my eyes: on the signal of the deputy group leader, everyone took a hold of their duvet and carefully placed it on the floor; they then rolled up their mattresses, sheets and all, and placed those on another spot on the floor. Everyone then pulled their real bedding out from under their beds and spread it out on an area of floor indicated by the group leader. But there was not enough space for everyone, and the short-term prisoners had to arrange themselves as three in a space for two. I sat watching this transformation, utterly amazed. Is there really no miracle that cannot be achieved under the leader-ship of the Chinese Communist Party? And among those people who participate in achieving these miracles are so many just accustomed and numb to the reality of what they do.

At dawn, after the duty-men had issued the order to get up, the group leaders spurred everyone on to get up and dressed in a matter of minutes. Everyone then rolled up their bedding and someone was assigned to make sure everything was again stuffed under the bed; they even stamped and kicked at the bedding rolls to try and make sure even the slightest corner of cloth didn't reveal itself. At the same time, several people busied themselves with carefully rolling up the mattresses that had been distributed for the visit the day before. A specially designated person received each of the mattresses as though he were receiving some sacred sacrificial object before disappearing to place it back in storage.

I was disgusted by this blatant falsehood and fabrication. I felt like ripping up the sheets in front of those bank workers. The reason I didn't was not because I was afraid of the consequences, but rather I didn't want to embarrass the prison. In front of all of those young men and women from the bank, it would have been mortifying for the staff. Instead, when the bank workers had left I presented my criticism of the falsehood in person to a prison official. A few days later, I submitted an even sterner criticism in writing.

I said that they were a legal institution supposedly specializing in 'reforming criminals' who then arranged for those selfsame subjects of reform to falsify and fabricate; therefore, this was surely a blatant negation of their very reason for being. Was this not dragging criminals yet further below the waves? I asked, how could it be that when China's economy is the fastest-growing in the world, the funds cannot even be found to supply prisoners with mattresses? If they couldn't be afforded, then at least allow prisoners to arrange for their own mattresses. Even if it required extra time and effort to get them into the prison, it would at least be infinitely better than these falsifications and fabrications.

The prison responded to my questions and criticism with silence. They had no other choice: they had no way of arguing, and they were too stuck in their vile ways.

As far as I'm aware, this farce of getting the mattresses out for the day and putting them away at night is still going on today.

And then there's the deaf man's ears – the library, which is never used. Has it ever been used by a prisoner? Has a prisoner ever borrowed a book? I later went to group three, where I met a prisoner who regularly went into the reading room to clean. He told me that the library was well stocked and even had some encyclopedias and beautifully bound books. But they had not been supplied for the prisoners to read nor to raise the prisoners' 'levels of spiritual civilization'. The books were there because they existed only as means to hoodwink. A library enables the transfer and dissemination of knowledge, and that is truly 'valuable'; but this library's true function had been suffocated.

In actual fact, the Chinese people deceive themselves far

more than once a year with an improvised performance on April Fool's Day; in reality, it happens day after day, year after year, a never-ending series of deceptions.

Translated by Ben Carrdus

Ali al-Dumaini

The Saudi writer and poet Ali al-Dumaini was arrested in March 2004 for criticizing the National Commission on Human Rights. Al-Dumaini subsequently refused to sign a pledge promising not to engage in further political activity on the grounds that pro-reform lobbying was in the interests of his country. He was charged with threatening 'national unity', and accused of promoting a constitutional monarchy and using Western terminology in his demands for more wide-ranging political reform. He was eventually sentenced to nine years in prison. After an International PEN campaign, and shortly after receiving the 2005 PEN/ Barbara Goldsmith Freedom to Write Award, al-Dumaini was granted a royal pardon on 8 August 2005.

Al-Dumaini's publications include three collections of poetry and a novel. While in prison, he wrote the first part of his memoirs, *Time for Prison, Times for Freedom*, which was published on 30 November 2004 in Beirut.

The following is an extract from al-Dumaini's memoirs, where he recalls the eighteen months he spent in prison in 1982 (on suspicion of being a member of the Communist Party), which were to have a formative influence on him.

Time for prison, times for freedom

I remained in the reception area for two hours since they had nowhere else to put me as the cells were full of people they had arrested the day before. When they were at their wits' end over what to do with me, they took me to a storeroom that was used for broken furniture and left a guard to sit with me.

'What are you charged with, boy?' asked the guard.

'I don't know. Perhaps they'll arrange something for me.'

'No, they don't bring anyone in without reason but you'd better prepare yourself to be tortured. God, I've just come back from seeing prisoners hanging from a fan and they were being whipped and tortured with electricity.'

I tried to remain calm and yawned so that he would not see how frightened I was. I had heard about vile practices such as these, which are carried out by secret police the world over. Other political prisoners had spoken about them. The late Sayyid Ali al-'Awami, for example, described a journey in open trucks from Dhahran to al-Ahsa prison during which the soldiers took turns in beating the prisoners until most of them lost consciousness; Abd al-Rahman al-Baheijan described how the soldiers used to spit on him and abuse him foully every time they passed his cell. It was only later when a guard explained that the interrogators wanted to spread the word that 'you fuck your sister', that he found out the reason for such gross behaviour.

'If you are accused of something, it's better to confess,' said the guard loudly.

'No, I've got no problem with the government. I'm just a writer and a poet.'

'A poet, are you? What do you say to letting me hear one of your poems now?'

'My poems are in classical Arabic and not easy to appreciate.'

'God help you, you're going to see things tonight you and your poems have never seen before.'

I didn't say anything and the guard moved outside, but when it was nearly nine o'clock in the evening, he took me out to a car and we went to another building, where I was photographed in my headscarf and had my fingerprints taken. After that I was taken to a modern building which housed the administration of the secret police of the Itisalat district. Today it's behind the al-Muajil apartment block, which wasn't built then.

Inside the building I found a large group of secret police going through my books, papers and other belongings. My heart contracted at the sight of the library which I had so painstakingly assembled in al-Baha, Jeddah, the College of Petroleum, Aramco and al-Doha district in Dhahran and during my travels to Kuwait, Baghdad, Amman, Damascus and Cairo.

I was devoted to my books; they were my lifelong companions. I'd scribbled comments in their margins or summarized them on bits of paper which were now scattered and tossed about the hall. Who would ensure they were returned to me later ...?

I was taken down to the basement, past posters on the walls which declaimed, 'Confess and you will save yourself' or 'Tell the truth and you will be saved'. The basement smelt of damp and heat although autumn had started. Water seeped out of the ground; the guards were taking it away in buckets to prevent us from drowning in it.

At one in the morning the guard took me to the interrogator's room. Ahmed Naher was a quiet man. He would throw out one question then surprise you with another which he had carefully prepared, when you were in the middle of answering the first.

Although he gained from the element of surprise, I was pleased at these supplementary questions because they got me out of details that I didn't want to go into ...

At about three o'clock in the morning, he asked me about the leaflets which they had found in my office.

'Can I look at them so I can answer your question?' I asked.

At that, he closed his interrogation book and ordered the guard to take me back to the cell. After I'd escaped Ahmed Naher's net,

I fell into such a sweet sleep as I've never experienced since, and didn't wake up till I heard Mohammed al-Ali and Mubarek al-Hamoud grunting in the neighbouring cells around noon.

[In subsequent interrogations in Dammam and Riyadh, Ahmed Naher's place was usually taken by his deputy, a man known as Abu Mansur.]

… I found out Abu Mansur's (real) name by chance, when a guard chucked cold water over me early one morning, while I was still asleep.

'Wake up, you're wanted by Sirah al-Ruwaili.'

When I sat down in front of his desk I knew from the angry expression on his face that he was determined to break me. He grasped his heavy stick and began to beat me. Pain flooded through my body. I got to my feet and he hit me in the stomach with the head of his stick so hard that I thought it had gone through to the other side. I didn't change my position.

He sat down on his chair and started speaking in a soft, changed voice, opening his book so that we could finish the interrogation. At about five o'clock in the morning, when I had finished answering his questions, he ordered the guard to take me back to my cell.

'Tomorrow you'll be meeting the lieutenant so prepare yourself.'

I was completely exhausted but I was unable to eat or sleep throughout the day. I sympathized with those other prisoners who had undergone interrogation or torture during the night and were now forced to shuffle about in chains for up to five days at a time. At seven o'clock in the evening, the guard knocked on my door and dragged me off to Abu Mansur.

Abnormally for him, Abu Mansur bid me welcome. He told me we were going to see the lieutenant, and that I should confess everything.

We went down the stairs to the third floor and into an office. Abd al-Aziz bin Masoud was an imposing man. He had an enormous moustache which was shot through with grey, a broad face and keen hawk-like eyes, which had a cruel glint in them. He told me to sit down by his desk. He placed a copy of the Qu'ran on it and beside it a revolver.

'We know that confessing the truth is difficult, but by the Great God of this book' – and he placed his hand upon it – 'I swear that if you don't confess the truth then we will extract it from you with this', and he placed his hand on the revolver.

My head spun. I almost put my hands up to it but tried to remain calm. 'Everything to do with me is written down in the interrogation book,' I said. 'I have nothing to add.'

He stared into my eyes. I somehow found the courage to return his gaze. He turned to Abu Mansur, who was skulking in a corner of the room, as if he was as frightened as I was, and ordered him to give me an exercise book and pen to take back to my cell, in which to write down all the details I could remember. Then he ordered me to leave. I followed Abu Mansur out into the long corridor. I told him I was not concealing anything and didn't need a notebook; if he wanted to continue his investigation then it should be in his office.

He agreed and ordered the guard to take me back to my cell. I felt revitalized like someone who has just that moment escaped from the grave. That night, at least, the lieutenant's threats had not materialized and I was happy. I was also pleased that I'd refused to take the interrogation booklet with me. In the past I'd felt frightened when I'd glanced through the hole in the door and seen comrades returning with those tattered notebooks.

Back in my cell I played with the ant I'd been feeding, which I'd named Wirda, and which had relieved my loneliness during the months of solitary confinement. I no longer needed to worry about being seen with a notebook, fearful that someone might think I was going to pass on information against them.

When you are alone in a cell you are subject to fancies and strange explanations. In reality, if someone wants to confess or is forced to confess then he will do so in front of the interrogator.

This incident affected me and I recorded the memory in a short poem which I learnt by heart and wrote down after I left prison.

> You will climb up the ladder, Sir,
> Whenever
> Your hands have restrained me
> Your chests will be weighed down with medals
> Whenever
> Your steps have brought pain to me
> But you will never forget, Sir,
> That it is
> I who have lifted you out of starvation,
> And placed you in your position.
> And after this, I won't forget you
> Or your frowning face
> When it is time for the accounts to be settled.
>
> (Prison of the Ministry of the Interior, Riyadh, 1982)

Two months went by during which I only slept once morning had arrived, fearful that Sirah al-Ruwaili would send for me while I was still asleep. I made myself remain awake until morning prayers then slept until it was time for midday prayers. The interrogators were busy with other people. They summoned me from time to time though they didn't get anything from me. I was a member of a background cell and was determined not to confess till the end. But once I was surprised by a question, which had been written down in the interrogation book and which I can still remember word for word.

'Tell us everything you know about Khaled al-Nuzha and which organization he belongs to. Give us the details.'

I told the interrogator that Khaled al-Nuzha was a close friend and that we had studied together but I didn't know which organization he belonged to.

He stared at my answer for a long time, his face clearly troubled, then ordered the guard to take me back to my cell.

(I thought, though I wasn't sure, that Khaled belonged to the Communist Party ... but I don't have the right or the proof to confirm that.)

After that I noticed that the number of guards had doubled; every half an hour, they peered at us through the small opening in the cell door usually used for passing food.

'Do you think we are going to escape through the ceiling?' I shouted at one of them.

'No, we're concerned about you. Do you want water or cigarettes?'

'No, thanks,' I said and closed the opening.

How could I have imagined that my friend was dead? He had died while being interrogated. I only found out later, after we had been delivered from the hands of Sirah and his fellow interrogators, and been set free.

Two facts lie before me. First, Khaled al-Nuzha did not confess to being a member of a party and because of that he was severely tortured; secondly, he died during the period of interrogation and was perhaps found dead in his cell.

He died an innocent man, as did many others before him such as Sa'ud al Muammar, Wasfi al-Madah and Abd al-Rahman al-Shamrani, yet they remain symbols of steadfastness and witnesses to the sacrifices made by patriots who are seeking to establish justice, freedom and democracy.

Translated by Judy Cumberbatch

Faraj Ahmad Bayrakdar

A poet and journalist, Faraj Ahmad Bayrakdar was arrested on 31 March 1987 by Syria's Military Intelligence on suspicion of membership of the Party for Communist Action. He was held incommunicado for almost seven years and suffered torture while in detention. He was finally brought before the Supreme State Security Court, and sentenced to fifteen years in prison on 17 October 1993. Bayrakdar was released on 16 November 2000, under an amnesty granted by the president, leaving jail fourteen months before the end of his fifteen-year sentence without obligation to renounce his political activities.

These are extracts from a long poem Bayrakdar wrote in Saydnaia prison between 1997 and 2000.

Mirrors of absence

These mirrors could have been
pure rain
or pure silence
But things were made of stone
The clinking of time and space
was bloodied
with what resembles madness
or gods

1

Thanks
for what has to go
Thanks
for what has to come
Thanks
for what succumbs to silence
and never returns
never

4

His heart is a bell
his body a church
eyes shut
upon a woman
wearing her sorrow
holding a mass of tears
for his return

7

They whispered:
who other than the madman
sharpens the rose
and is merciful to the knife?
O Khadija, the lamps of your sadness!
If you only knew
how many roses
and how many knives
I tore apart
and how many
tore me apart

9

There is no freedom
outside this place
but it cries
whenever it hears keys
laughing in their locks

10

All the cracks you see on the wall
were carved by my eyes
they have been looking at them
for years
No use counting them

11

A time
without dates
A place
without directions
O woman
wounding like lightning
bleeding like a song
Go!
Nothing is present
except absence

12

Thus
prison is time

you mark the first days on walls
the following months on memory
but when you become
a long train
tired of whistling
despairing of a station
you try something else:
forgetting

16

There is no sun here
I find myself naked
without shades
no woman either
I find myself naked
without myself

18

O
How can I see myself
when I am always with me?
How do I know myself
Do not say no to the mirror!
Mirrors,
even the ones I write
can only enumerate me
or make me one
I am not like that
I am in no state
whatsoever

23

'Whose funeral procession is this?'
I asked the old man
'It is for meaning, my son'
he replied
and stood there
like a headstone

29

Here
and there
on the wall
on my heart
on the night and wind
on doors, dates and sidewalks
on fear, despair and nothingness
Eyes
deep like blackness
black like catastrophe
catastrophic like silence
silent like howling
nothing before or after them
except fallen banners,
God and I
in adjacent cells

30

Eleven harvested deserts
without a woman's shadow
four thousand blind nights

without a blink for the morning
a hundred thousand bleeding hours
with nothing but thorns, sand and scorpions
six million gasps
on a knife's edge
and the match goes on bloody and mad
between the wolves of death
and the gazelles of life

31

Yes O God!
this is Syria
how shall we raise
condolences to you
with which clouds will you cry?

34

Now I am forty-six dances old
on the brink of the abyss
my poems don't express me
any more than an arrow
expresses its prey

35

No
not God
but a woman
the colour of wheat and carob
a woman
between coffee and milk

between silence and speech
she taught me the rose in the morning
and before the night climbed
taught me the storm

37 ·

Freedom is a homeland
and my country an exile
I am my antithesis
this is my deposition
written with my mother's milk
stamped with all my chains

38

I hide inside the poem
search for myself outside
but we cheat at times
she invites me to her bed
I respond
she takes off her clothes
I, mine
she puts me on
and I remain naked

40

It is neither bias
nor bragging
there is no graveyard
in this world or the next
bigger than this one:

what I call
my country

41

What happens
when they open the gates?
What happens
when they shut them?
As if a heavy glass sky
is ripped from its seventh heaven
Its fall grinds ears
nothing but the bubbles of silence
and the rattle
in time's throat

42

If I don't even own myself
why shouldn't I bank
on the impossible?

43

In a year
or two
ten or twenty
freedom will put on
her miniskirt
and receive me
Yes!
her colourful miniskirt
I don't like to see her

In mourning

46

In the middle of forgetfulness
or at its end
my memory eloped towards her
She who initially uttered an absolute sky
and two obscure violets
a mirage-bleeding desert
but silence after silence
and breath after breath
she uttered my body
and a stormy sea
cried, rained and screamed
from the depths:
Come!

47

Blessed are you woman
I have no wings
how shall I draw space?
I have no space
what would I do with wings?

53

My body was filled with
swallows and larks
bee-eaters and herons
sand grouses, seagulls and eagles
but whenever I passed a walkway

a bird would fall off
here I am on the last shore
without a single bird

57

Her mouth smiles
her eyes teary
she calls out
in the photograph:
Daddy!

68

After a gasp or two
after a cup full of nostalgia
spilling and broken
After a god
a dog
or a tyrant
my mother will fold
fourteen skies
after my absence

74

Black mirrors
cannot see
White mirrors
cannot remember
Faded mirrors
the colour of neutrality
O woman of rain

I wish my heart were made of basalt!

78

Scientists and priests,
historians and philosophers,
fortune-tellers, leaders and sages,
religions,
parties,
and armies
but no truth

90

Mirrors cry
wipe their tears
and cover me O woman
with what is not absence

92

Four cigarettes
I wish I could smoke them all at once:
birth
love
freedom
and death
O good jailer:
Come let us smoke!
and continue our conversation

93

A little while ago
I squeezed an orange
like my heart
I added some burning alcohol
like the past
I took a deep breath
I lit a long and slender cigarette
whose smoke is like the memory
of a woman I once knew
then I smiled
to surprise myself
Good evening O life
Good evening friends
Good evening to myself
I invited you tonight
to inaugurate the fifteenth year
since my imprisonment
Who amongst you
will cut this ribbon
of barbed wire?
Do not blame me for my sadness!
I am not sad for myself
I am just in pain
So many are born now
I wish to drink to their health
and cry
In nostalgia

99

I entered prison
fully prepared
for death
Here I am
after – I don't know how many years
I arrange my dreams to leave
fully prepared for life

100

The birds
which I release
when I shut my eyes
The gazelles
which I follow to the spring
when I shut my eyes
The slopes
whose echoes I wipe
when I shut my eyes
The handkerchiefs
I embroider with stars
when I shut my eyes
The roses
I pluck from my heart
when I shut my eyes
are all:
Good Morning Freedom!

Saydnaia Prison 1997–2000

Translation by Sinan Antoon

Asiye Güzel

Asiye Güzel, a former editor of a socialist Turkish newspaper, was arrested in February 1997, accused of involvement in an 'illegal' organization. She spent five years in untried detention, until her release in June 2002, pending the final decision of the Supreme Court on her case. In October 2002 she was sentenced *in absentia* to a 12½-year prison term on the basis of a trial that fell short of international standards of fairness. By then she had left Turkey for Sweden, where she was a recipient of the Tucholsky Award. Asiye remains in Sweden, where she was granted asylum.

While in custody she committed evidence of rape and torture to paper, and the resulting diaries were smuggled out and made into a book – published, extraordinarily, while she was still in prison in Turkey. Asiye's Story was published in English translation by Saqi Books in 2003.

Asiye's story

'Hey, Asiye, what's up?' one man said.

Then he continued: 'Why are you going around with someone else's identity card?'

'I am the features editor of the *Workers' Path* newspaper. Since I have been charged I carry this identity card.'

Then someone else came into the room. He was a tall man with fair hair.

'Do you take us for fools? What do you think these are that we found in your flat?'

'What do you mean?' I asked, looking at the various false documents that were laid out in front of me. I replied, 'There was nothing like that in our flat, they don't belong to us,' and as I said that I was slapped heavily by someone at my side. Was my jaw broken, I wondered?

'I want to get in touch with my lawyer and family.'

They laughed, and inside myself I wanted to laugh too. Such a request was truly comic for the situation I was in.

They put pen and paper on the table. One of the policemen, whom I presumed to be the leader, said: 'Sit down and write.' He put down a few identity cards and photos which he had in his hand, and pointed at them.

'Look, this one stays with you, this one comes and goes,' he started to say, and added: 'Don't mess with us, sit down and write.'

'I've nothing to write.'

'You know best.'

We were eye to eye and his didn't blink.

'Take her away and let her think a bit.'

They put on the blindfold tightly again. I was taken to what was probably the same place as before.

Again I was left with myself. The silence there became terrifying.

What time was it, I wondered. Had my husband come home? Why were they keeping me waiting? While I was lost in thought, wondering why they hadn't taken me to be tortured, a very strong hand suddenly grabbed my arm. I was taken again to the same room. They took off the blindfold.

'Nilgun, have you thought about it?'

Nilgun ... But there wasn't anybody else in the room being held. He was talking to me, trying to disorient me.

'There's nothing to think about.'

'You'll be sorry, don't crush yourself, you'll see, you won't stand it ...'

'I've got nothing to say.'

'Leave them all, take this one first.'

They put on the blindfold again. I felt remarkably calm. We started to walk; the men were composed. It was obvious that they were used to doing this. They were as calm as I was.

'Take your top off and leave the rest on,' a voice shouted from behind.

We went up in the lift. There was a concrete floor in the room to which I was taken. I could make this out from under the blindfold; there was nothing laid on the floor.

'Do you want to strip off or shall we do it?'

I stripped myself so they wouldn't touch my body.

I took off my scarf, sweater and T-shirt, and they sat me in a chair. I had never experienced suspension torture, but I guessed from what I had heard and read and what I knew of the procedures that it was now going to happen. They tied my arms to a wooden beam, and finally they finished. Hoopla, I was hanging. At first I said to myself: 'Hey, is this what they call hanging?' Initially one feels no pain at all. After some time, however, I started feeling sharp pains in my armpits. But they couldn't hold out for long, and let me down. My arms were numb, but I could still feel them. Two of the men were moving them around to make the numbness go away. Then they took off the rest of my clothes: my trousers, socks and underclothes. I wasn't in a position to oppose them. My arms were tied tightly behind me. They put them through the wooden beam. Suddenly I was up in the air again, and this time the pain was more acute. My attempts at breathing turned into another torture. My ribcage seemed to be bursting. There were no questions. No one talked, only voices that said: 'OK? Enough?' I was on the ground again. My arms had no sensation now. I was naked and my nakedness frightened me. I was ashamed – I, who felt uncomfortable if my skirt was a bit short, was naked in front of all these men.

They had taken down all my defences. My husband came into my mind. I had to think of other things. I tried to sing a song to myself. Damn it, nothing came to mind. I had forgotten all the songs I ever knew. I tried to remember one line, one verse. The only thing on my mind was my nakedness:

You're naked!

'*That's OK, I knew that would happen.*'

But you're naked. You've got nothing on.

I didn't know how many people there were in the room – I couldn't work it out from their voices and they didn't talk much.

You're naked!

'*That's alright. They aren't human beings.*'

I was sweating, sweating profusely as though bucket after bucket of water had been poured on me.

I had to think of something else.

You're naked in front of so many men, what are you thinking, you're naked! They can do to you whatever they want. Ask for your clothes.

I wasn't alone, someone inside me was speaking. We were fighting. Asiye had started fighting with Asiye.

You're naked. You've no protection.

'Let it be, I knew this would happen'

But you're naked. Ask for your clothes, go on, ask for them.

The men in the room are looking at you, ask for your clothes. Don't let them touch you, let them give you your clothes back. Don't ask for anything else, just your clothes. If they touch you, what will you say to your husband?

He knows that you could experience this. Both of you could have guessed this could happen. What could he say? But what if he would never want to be with you again, what if he felt disgusted with you?

If you don't ask for your clothes he will hate you. Go on, ask for your clothes.

I was in another world. I couldn't hear the questions,

insults, swear words. They took me down again. My arms were not mine; I couldn't feel them.

Let them give me back my clothes, I pleaded silently. I didn't want anything else. On my mind were only my trousers, my sweater, my scarf. I was locked onto them.

More suspension followed.

Why don't you ask for your clothes, they are your armour, your shell. Ask for them!

'No, it'll all be over soon. They'll give them back then.'

They won't give them back if you don't ask for them. The quicker you put them on the better it'll be. You shouldn't stay naked any longer. Everyone is looking at you, examining you, observing you. Ask for your trousers.

Ask for your sweater.

Ask for your clothes.

Ask for them, time's passing, get on with it.

I had forgotten all the songs I knew and loved. I couldn't remember anyone's face, even those I loved most. There must be one, I thought, they couldn't be so distant ... I had to find a place to hold on to.

You're alone! There's no one to hold on to. Ask for your clothes. Ask for them, what more are you waiting for? They'll protect you.

I heard the door open. Some new person must have come in.

'Aren't you through yet? What are you trying to do? Let her down and lay her on the ground, the whore.'

Let her down and lay her on the ground?

I was let down from suspension. I couldn't stand, I couldn't feel my arms or control them. The pain was terrific. They threw me to the ground. After my head hit the ground, I felt the icy concrete. I was pouring sweat. I tried to use my arms to get on my feet, but I couldn't get through to them. I heard laughter and swear words. I tried to cover my nakedness, but couldn't. The thought came to mind that they would give me a beating there and then. I couldn't comprehend anything, I could only make out glimpses of their feet under my blindfold. I decided to give up trying to get to my feet, but tried to get my legs working. Their kicking stopped me. They held on tightly to my arms and legs. My efforts to struggle free were in vain. I tried to shout but no sound emerged.

'No, you can't do that – murder me, tear me apart but don't touch me. Don't dirty me, don't stain me!' I wanted to say. Everything was happening so fast, I was ready to go crazy. I felt a heaviness upon me. My teeth were clenched with the pain. I couldn't resist or move at all, not even get my mind to work. My throat was going to tear apart from screaming. My shouts, screams, my voice even seemed alien to me. The laughter and foul swearing never stopped. They were saying horrible things.

One of them said: 'Even your husband didn't manage this.'

When that horrible heaviness on me had finished its business, I felt frozen as water turned to ice. I was frozen like a mummy. Even my wish to die was taken away from me.

Suddenly everywhere went dark. There wasn't a single light. I was in the dark. A pitch-black darkness like infinity. Everything, everyone had passed one by one to the other side of darkness. I was left alone. There was no one to stretch my hand out to, to hold it. I became aware that the heaviness on me had lifted. When it lifted it took my soul with it.

I couldn't recall my mother's face, or my father's, the faces of those I loved. I was rolling down into an abyss. I had been dirtied, I wouldn't be able to look anyone in the face, wouldn't be able to love, wouldn't be able to be a mother. I had nothing left to live for, they had taken everything away. I was lost in a vacuum.

When I came to I was lying in a chair; they had given back my clothes. I hugged them to me. There was no one in the room.

My eyes weren't blindfolded. I wanted to get to my feet but my body wouldn't allow it. I was like a corpse. I couldn't work out where reality began and ended. Someone came into the room and I tried to get up but couldn't.

'Do you want anything?'

I wanted some water, but no sound came out. I couldn't open my mouth.

He went out of the room. I just wanted to sleep, so that I wouldn't be here when I woke up ... so that I wasn't dirtied, so that I was clean. Fever was pressing on me from all sides but I was cold. I hugged my clothes to me even tighter.

I slept. I woke and I was still there. Curses, a thousand curses. This was a dream, a nightmare. Then why didn't it end? I had to sleep, to sleep, so this nightmare would end, so my loved ones would come and awaken me, saying, 'Wake up now, you've slept too long, that's enough.' I was waiting; why didn't anyone come? I was going crazy; this nightmare had no end. I had no concept of time. Two men came into the room. They held me under the arms and lifted me. I couldn't stand. My feet and legs did not seem to belong to me – they were like a doll's limbs. They held me by the arms and took me to another room. They gave me a cigarette, but I had given up smoking. But how I wanted one then! I accepted the cigarette, thinking that it might help me get my head together. I took a couple of puffs and my head started to spin. No one spoke. There was only that accursed silence. How long had I been here? When did I come here? I didn't know, I couldn't remember.

There was a piece of yellowish, cheap paper and a pen on the table. They offered me the pen and I took it. What would I do then, what would I write? I wanted to sleep, I couldn't stand it, my eyelids felt they were lifting a weight of many tons.

And I started writing ... But it was as though the hand that wrote were not mine. I was watching it from another place, I couldn't say 'don't write'. Even if I said it, I wouldn't have heard it. I was so far from myself. If I had shouted out at the top of my lungs, or screamed, no one would have heard me.

Everything was on the other side of the darkness. I was completely alone; the other Asiye who had talked to me was not there. She had upped and gone ...

Translated by Richard McKane

Augusto Ernesto Llosa Giraldo

Peruvian, Augusto Ernesto Llosa Giraldo, a former journalist for Radio Casma and director of the newspaper *El Casmeno*, was arrested on 14 February 1995 and was sentenced to six years' imprisonment. This was later reduced to five years and further charges were dismissed.

Llosa Giraldo was accused of being a witness to a terrorist act in Cuzco in 1986. After failing to show up for the hearing he was charged with contempt of court. Police reportedly went through documents in his home as part of their investigation. Among these were documents belonging to the Peruvian Journalists' Association seeking the release of jailed reporters.

The police statement reported that Llosa Giraldo had not been involved in the attacks and that he was not in Cuzco at the time. Other evidence against him included witness statements and letters, which were reportedly not corroborated. On the basis of this investigation it was initially decided not to prosecute him. The decision was overturned by the prosecutor's office and, with no further evidence against him, he was convicted of terrorism. Llosa Giraldo was released in February 2000 on completion of a five-year sentence.

The following is his account of an unusual prison visit.

'Chiquitín'

Fiery rays seemed to split the day asunder, while noisy raindrops ceaselessly pounded on this adoptive land which reached out to us, while causing those ill prepared to suffer its sometimes devastating effects to flee.

The main entrance door was slightly ajar where the security guards grouped in a little surveillance hut, located to the side of the enormous prison building; it was under these circumstances that 'Chiquitín', an old mongrel dog soaked by the rain and terrified by the thunder, silently entered the Political Prisoners' Section, without anyone noticing or restraining him.

Finding himself inside the prison precincts, he began sniffing around in search of food, and was well received by the inmates; some called him by various names, while others tried to grab him in order to pet him, but he behaved fearfully, never having received this kind of attention in the past; still others proffered food, such as dried fish, to him. He ate everything, and managed to finally sate his canine voracity while remaining at a prudent distance. We were all cheered by the first such unusual visit in years: but night inevitably fell, when the screws began to lock all the barred gates in the different sections, and 'Chiquitín', as we baptized him, remained trapped as one more prisoner in the concentric structure of this enormous and sinister place.

Hours passed, and when most of the inmates were asleep, suddenly the dog began to bark and to race desperately up and down all the corridors in the section, letting out a succession of heart-rending howls.

This continued until he finally stopped at the barred front gate, unleashing a lacerating cry that tore us all apart. There was nothing for us to do but call on the guards stationed outside to put the hound out on the street so that we could all get some sleep.

And so it was, the head security guard gave the starting order for the inmates to call the screws with one voice; after a few minutes of loud and repeated yelling, they all came rushing in, convinced there was some medical emergency. They were greatly surprised to learn that they had been summoned to 'liberate' a dog, and could find no way at all of explaining how it had succeeded in penetrating somewhere normally inaccessible to any human, given the panoply of safety measures on which the most secure prison in the country depended.

The prisoners were moved by the dog's behaviour; nobody spoke afterwards – and the silence was eloquent.

That night many of the inmates dreamed of Liberty. I was among them.

Translated by Amanda Hopkinson

Mamadali Makhmudov

Mamadali Makhmudov is a well-known Uzbek writer and opposition activist who was arrested on 19 February 1999. He was sentenced to fourteen years in prison. It is thought that his detention is linked to his association with the exiled opposition leader Muhammed Salih, together with his writings and distribution of *Erk*, the newspaper of the opposition Erk party, banned in 1994. At the trial, Makhmudov testified to having been tortured during interrogation, alleging that he had been beaten, electrocuted and threatened with the rape of female family members.

Makhmudov is a writer of the traditional *dastan* style of epic verse, which typically features a hero with magical qualities. Under the Soviet Union, the *dastan* was said to be 'impregnated with the poison of feudalism' and Makhmudov was forced to repudiate his work. After the Soviet Union collapsed his most famous work, *Immortal Cliffs,* was retrospectively awarded the Cholpan Prize.

Makhmudov was hospitalized in July 2000, seemingly for facial and throat surgery, as a result of extreme ill-treatment and neglect in the Jaslyk camp where he was previously held. At the time of writing, he remains in prison.

This is an edited version of a letter from Mamadali Makhmudov, written in Chirchik prison, and smuggled outside in 2002.

Dear Friend,

In Navoi city prison I saw Rashid [Begzhan, Salih's brother and Makhmudov's co-defendant], and we met several times in secret. He was tortured all the time. I tried to help him, although I needed help myself. I could have been killed on the slightest of pretexts. So I had to be careful. They endlessly, constantly, tortured those prisoners who had been convicted under Article 159 [Infringement of the Constitutional Order of the Republic of Uzbekistan].

From early morning to evening they made us crawl, run, sing the national anthem; they threw us into the psychiatric ward etc. There were serial murderers who had killed six people apiece, but they were barely mistreated.

Rashid's arms, legs and face were chapped. He withered and shrank in front of my eyes.

I lost consciousness twice in the courtyard and later the doctors said, 'It's rare that anyone in that condition survives.'

But God apparently did not want my death, because I am still breathing.

I wrote a series of poems ... I wrote a novel, unfinished, which was smuggled to the outside ... I am now writing a novel in verse.

On the night of 23 April 2001 they dragged me to the attendant's room. There, sitting sadly in the corner, a ghost of his former self, was Muhammad [Begzhan, Salih's brother and a co-defendant with Makhmudov]. When I saw him, I wanted to cry.

Then the two of us were taken to the train by a huge number of cops, armed to the teeth, complete with guard dogs. As I got on the train, I was hit on the head by a truncheon. Everything went dark. There were eighty prisoners, arrested under Article 159, on the train. All of them young men.

There was nowhere to sit. There was no water. Our clothes became wet. There was no toilet, we defecated into polythene bags.

Stench.

It was impossible to breathe.

And still they hit us. And yelled, 'Enemies of the people! Traitors to the homeland!'

And so, under a rain of truncheon-beatings and insults, we arrived at the Jaslyk death camp on 24 April.

Jaslyk is located 380 kilometres away from Nukus, on Barsa Kelmes island. Although they call it a 'zone' [camp], it's a closed colony with prison cells.

I lost all my writings, my glasses, pen, soap, toothbrush, clothing there ...

As we entered the zone, the cops fell upon us. They had truncheons, steel pipes ... they began to hammer us.

We lay scattered, everywhere blood, blood.

Some had their legs broken, some had their skulls fractured, some were just outright killed.

A constant wailing surrounded us.

I was hit with a steel pipe and lost consciousness.

When I came to, I saw that I was lying naked on the second floor [of the prison]. And I thought of Muhammad, of whether he was alive.

Then they dragged us to the cells, still naked.

I didn't see Muhammad. I kept worrying about him.

The cell doors were thirty to forty centimetres thick, and inside the cell was a three-layer steel grate.

You had to get permission to go to the toilet.

We weren't allowed to lift our heads. If we did, we'd be beaten to a pulp.

They beat us anyway. They beat us for no reason. They kicked us and yelled, 'Traitor to the homeland, enemy of the people!'

They used force to make us adopt the thirteen positions. (It's said that they're based on Mossad techniques).

The first position is: The prisoners must declaim in a chorus, '*Assalomu alaiku*, Citizen Chief, we love the President of Uzbekistan and the Uzbek people from the bottom of our hearts, we ask forgiveness of the President of Uzbekistan and the Uzbek people. Thank you to the Chief, food is good, health is good, everything is great!'

We had to repeat this refrain 500 times a day. Then we had to sing anthems in Uzbek and Karakalpak, hundreds of times! We were forced to crawl naked.

Boys fell like flies, some fainted. I myself almost died there several times.

The food we were given was leftovers, one loaf of bread for six people. And we were fed under the truncheon ...

In my opinion, 80–90 per cent of the prisoners there suffered from tuberculosis. And I think that everyone's insides were rotting.

You can't fit all of this into one book.

The cops said, 'This is the Titanic, no one escapes from here alive,' and beat us constantly.

In two months, I lost twenty-four kilos. Then, apparently under pressure from the international community and my relatives' rallying to my cause, I was transported to Navoi. In the train a young boy named Abdulkarim died, and I held him. We travelled from Jaslyk to Navoi in a Black Maria [secure police van]. With people suffering from tuberculosis.

I thought, who are these people, who gave birth to them? A dog or a wolf? A snake or a fox? I can't believe that anyone could be capable of such brutality. No one knows how many people have died in Jaslyk. Many die every day at the sanatorium ...

'Stability', 'Peace', all of that is a lie. When will this mob become human? The people are hungry and naked. Science and agriculture have died out. Depravity is everywhere. Everything – riches, the press, radio and television, publishing – everything serves one person only.

In Navoi I saw Rashid again. I cried. In the toilet I gave him rolling tobacco and bread. Then Rashid was shipped off to Kiziltepe. It might be easier there, I thought.

I lay in the hospital for sixteen days. They put me on an IV, once I lost consciousness, they thought I was dying, but God gave me life and I opened my eyes again. Five prisoners died in six days.

Then I was sent to Navoi again. Muhammad [Salih's brother] and I were in the same zone. We talked non-stop. I was on relatively good terms with the Chief and so was able to make Muhammad's life a bit easier, lessen the humiliation and beatings he faced. We supported each other.

Then he was thrown into another division. He crushed stones from morning to night. I sometimes secretly sent him food. His leg was broken during a beating. He suffered horribly from the pain in his leg. I told the Chief that the 'rats' [informers] broke his leg, and asked that he be freed from working; the Chief called him in and promised to ease his workload, but didn't want to release him from working altogether.

We heard rumours that people from the Red Cross would be visiting. All at once everything was being renovated. Each prisoner arrested under 159 was warned that if he said anything he'd be punished severely, killed, etc.

Two thousand prisoners were hurriedly removed to other zones. The three-level bunk beds disappeared, everyone was given new sheets and towels. In short, a total put-up job!

Suddenly, on 11 April 2001, I alone was sent to Sangorod. Before my departure, I told the Chief that Muhammad had been beaten up again. As I was leaving, he was being brought in, we saw each other in the corridor, but the cop in charge didn't allow us to say goodbye. I haven't seen my Muhammad, my brother, since then.

They found an ulcer and polyps in my intestine. I have asthma and bronchitis, hypertension and have had three heart attacks! Haemorrhoids and many other different illnesses. They wanted to operate on my stomach, but decided that my heart couldn't bear the strain and got an official refusal from the head doctor and Chief. In actual fact I should have received Invalid, First Category status. But an order came down from above. All they did was write on my hospital card that I should be relieved of all work. I found out that much can be done here for money. I needed a lot of money. But where could I get it? My son could barely feed me. They were asking for a lot of money ... At that moment, because of something published on the internet, they decided to deport me. I wrote an official request asking to be sent to Chirchik. After discussing the matter, on 16 June 2001 I was sent here. Chirchik is relatively better. If you have money, you can do something. I work with all my strength. Five or six days ago Khamid Ismailov [journalist with the BBC World Service based in London] came to me, you can listen to the BBC and hear everything he has to say for yourself.

The oppression increased when The Vile One [President Karimov] returned from America. An order came from on high to torture the 159-ers [those imprisoned under Article 159]. Each day ten people are taken away. I was on yesterday's list ... I refused. Today is a bit quieter.

The prisons are overflowing, 99 per cent of the prisoners are young. There are hundreds of thousands of them.

Dear friend! I wrote this letter to you in one sitting, in a hurry, I was very tired. I didn't have time to read it over again, having asked one of my trustworthy friends to stand guard. I have described only one of the thousand thoughts swirling about in my soul. I apologize for my mistakes. I greet you, miss you, and embrace you, wish you the greatest from God.

22 April 2002

Unofficial translation by Human Rights Watch

Yndamiro Restano

The Cuban poet and founder of the Independent Journalists' Association Yndamiro Restano was arrested in December 1991 in Havana. In May 1992, he was sentenced to ten years in prison for 'rebellion'. He was also accused of 'preparing printed material inciting civil disobedience and actions against socialist society' and distributing counter-revolutionary propaganda. He was released on 1 June 1995.

The following poem was written in November 1993.

Prison

Mother,
do you know where your poet is?
Well, they have dragged me into a dark,
narrow, lonely cell.
And do you know why,
Mother?
For not allowing fear to carry me away.

But I am not completely alone,
Mother.
I have got to know a good friend here.
A small spider visits me every day
and spins in the door of my cell.
When the guard comes,

I let it know so it hides away
and doesn't get killed.

I want it to live,
Mother,
Because I know that it has inside it
something that I also possess.
However,
it seems that the guard does not know this.

Mother,
Do you know where your poet is?
Well, they have dragged me to a cold,
narrow, lonely cell.
And do you know why,
Mother?
Because the poet is the only person
who never forgets
the meaning of freedom.

Translated by Mandy Garner

The following is a letter from Restano to his English PEN minder.

To Rod Wooden:
I am the creative mirror
which creates you.
I am the sorceress mirror
where you dance when you see
that everything has the sense
that we give it.
I am the magical mirror

and so are you.
And we are experts in understanding,
experts in knowing
that if it is possible to leave,
it is possible to return.
I am the creative mirror
which creates you
with the expressive language of the light.

Translated by Maria Delgado

Faraj Sarkohi

The writer and editor Faraj Sarkohi signed a petition in 1994 calling for greater freedom of expression in Iran. He was arrested in September 1996, but was later released without charge. On 4 November 1996, en route to visit his wife in Germany, the editor 'disappeared'. According to the German authorities he had never arrived, but the Iranian official newspaper reported that he had boarded the plane. Sarkohi finally reappeared in Tehran airport on 20 December 1996 and gave an interview to the national and international press stating that he had gone to Germany in order to obtain custody of his children. In January 1997, a letter was published in which Sarkohi claimed that he had not left Iran in November, but had been held by Iranian Intelligence Services, and that he had been tortured.

Sarkohi was rearrested in January 1997 and held in untried detention for nine months. He was initially to go on trial for 'espionage', but the charges were later changed to 'propaganda against the Islamic Republic of Iran'. Sarkohi was sentenced on 17 September 1997 to one year in prison. After an international campaign was mounted on his behalf, he was released from prison on 28 January 1998.

The following is an edited extract from Sarkohi's novel, recalling his own disappearance and imprisonment. A man finds himself possessed by the spirit of a former political prisoner, known only as number 612. Another voice contradicts 612, giving a palpable sense of a never-ending interrogation.

We make death easy

... It was clear from the discoloured leaves of the ancient plane tree in the photograph that it must have been an autumn evening, like all the other autumn evenings on which 612 had been arrested. And you could see through the black eyes of the girl standing on the pavement in that nameless street that 612 was disappearing, on the orders of three security agents, into a black Mercedes, with darkened windows and a fake numberplate, so that he could be driven blindfolded through the crowded streets of Tehran, arriving at a workshop where they make death easy using simple, primitive instruments:

A cell measuring three by two. A black blindfold. A long, endless corridor. The torture chamber with a large photograph of the great shah or the imam of all times. A cable to be used for the beatings. A metal handcuff to be suspended by or with which to be tied to the torture bed. A metal bed to attach the victim to during the beatings. A wooden box measuring one by one in which the prisoner can experience the claustrophobia of the coffin. A rope to be hung by. Metal bars to be suspended from. Steel cuffs to fasten hands with behind the back. Weights for attaching to testicles. Pliers for removing fingernails. An iron for burning the buttocks and back. Horny men for fucking girls. A metal rod for inserting into the anuses of unattractive boys. Powerful fists to keep victims awake and ... 'We make death easy. We guide you over the threshold of death. We pulverize you. We make you disappear. We build you anew. We re-create you. Our work is artistic in nature. Our success is guaranteed.'

The man who had been possessed by 612 looked out of the small window of flight 824 from Stockholm to Hamburg. Through the clouds, which were not thick enough to impede the view, he could see the frozen lakes and mountains below. The icy megaliths invoked monsters out of some epic tale, frozen for all eternity by a wrathful god as they'd reached up their claws in a ferocious bid to rip the sky. That thwarted final wish was no more than a dream to them now, repeating endlessly in their frozen heads like some meaningless litany.

Who are you now?

The man was recalling the most recent event in his life: the night before. The party arranged by Swedish PEN. A ceremony for awarding the Tucholsky prize to 612. The emotional speech by Monica Nagler, the spokeswoman for Swedish PEN. The kind faces. Happy, friendly looks. The man had had no choice but to recount the tale of 612's three journeys, to speak of the burning, bitter secret and to explain that 612 had lost his body on the last journey, in the seventh circle of darkness, and that he'd become possessed by an antiquated spell that had taken hold of him …

'No, I didn't say that. I said that the pain always begins before the first lash of the cable makes contact with the skin. First they tie the feet to the bed. With each blow on the bare feet, tiny nerve cells transfer the pain – with the phenomenal precision of ancient astronomers, travelling through a terrifying storm at the speed of light – from the skin, muscles, bones, fat and veins to the brain. The sensation administered by the cables to the swollen feet surpasses the brain's threshold of pain. The head grows bigger and bigger. The eyes throb with pain and grow until, at bursting point, they try to leap out of their sockets. The lower jaw twists to the left. With each stroke, the shrieking of the cable rips the air like the flapping wings of a sharp-clawed eagle. A dry, heavy pain bends the tiny bones of the ears. The arms, which have been handcuffed to the bed on either side, stretch with each blow and as the excruciating stretching persists the fatigued muscles become paralysed. The ribs press against the chest to bursting point. The heart beats at an inconceivable pace. The kidneys and the bladder lose all control and warm urine and blood soil the trousers. The pain communicated from the soles of the feet to the rest of the body prepares the mind for the preaching of the interrogators and sermonizers. The tongue breaks open into pleas. Servility and shame cast their heavy shadow. The victim is crushed. "The cable opens the closed tongue. When the mouth is shut, the feet speak. When the mind is shut, the cable opens it."'

'I'm guilty. I'm a traitor, I'm a wretch, I'm a coward. I'm ...'

A moment's hesitation in the flurry of blows, a cigarette, a smile, a glass of cold water, a kind word appear like a glimpse of a godly–fatherly being, signs from gods–interrogators who hold life and death, pain and relief, sleep and sleeplessness in their powerful hands and who punish the misguided, unruly child to show him the path to salvation and bliss. 'We make death easy. We guide you over the threshold of death. We pulverize you. We make you disappear. We build you anew. We re-create you. Our work is artistic in nature. Our success is guaranteed.'

Who are you now?

'No, that's not what I said. I said that, at four o'clock in the morning on 3 November 1996, it was the fiftieth birthday of a man who had been running for half a century and had never arrived. Mehrabad airport, Tehran. I was a departing passenger. From Tehran to Hamburg. On an aircraft of the Islamic Republic of Iran which bears the emblem "Allah" and Allah doesn't like to see people fly. With two suitcases full of gifts. Books, shoes and clothes. A doll for my daughter. A pair of shoes for my son. Grinning pistachios from Damghan. Rosewater from Shiraz, with the scent of wild flowers from mountain fields. Nougat from Isfahan. Aromatic herbs from Tehran. A silk shirt. Two unfinished stories ... And two photographs. At the airport, there were three agents waiting for me.'

'No, that's not what you said. You said that one of the agents had lost an eye in the eight-year-long war with Iraq and that, despite his glass eye, he was still waiting for the day when he would liberate the holy shrine in Iraq and step across its threshold as a pilgrim.'

'No, that's not what I said. You must have read it somewhere or heard it from someone and are adding it to the story to entertain the readers. I said that one of Haj Asghar's eyes was made of glass. The one who had a talent for the beatings. I said that the steady look in Haj Asghar's glass eye was more telling and more human than his good eye. I said that there was only ever a frozen glare in his good green eye, but that his green glass eye cried out in grief for his brother's death in the sacred war. I said that he'd been a boxer when he was young and that one blow from his fist was enough to rob you of sleep for an eternity because of the chronic, relentless ache in your ribs.'

'You've grown fond of your executioners. I'd read it in books, that victims grow fond of their executioners.'

'You're not a judge. No one is a judge.'

'But you said that interrogators issue a sentence for each person and they prepare the person's file on the basis of that sentence in order to make things easy for each prisoner. You said that Majid Hashemi, who was the head interrogator and was an expert at beating people with a cable, used to convey a person's sentence to them after the first five blows.'

'I said that Majid Hashemi hated students, writers, girls and beautiful women, and whenever he raped women prisoners he'd cover their faces with a piece of cloth bearing verses from the Koran. I said that Majid Hashemi had had nineteen years of experience in beating people but that he'd still get tired on occasion. I said that Hashemi used to weep when he performed his daily prayers and that he used to pray for all prisoners and sinners. I said that Hashemi didn't like prison and that he used to take his old mother to the park in his free time.'

'But you try to justify the executioners' behaviour. You said that Haj Hosseini used to sit on a leather chair in the torture chamber perfectly calm and relaxed. You said that Haj Asghar and Hashemi used to take it in turns to beat people and when they felt tired they'd read the Koran, which is the word of God and calls on Muslims to murder and lynch the infidels.'

'No, I never said any of these things. You're making them up to add to my story ...'

I said that death is destroyed on the other side of darkness.

'But death has followed you from the seventh circle of darkness to Sweden. The one who is sitting behind me has poison in his eyes and a scythe in his pocket. You said that you'd known death since you were twenty, but you didn't recognize him the moment you needed to.'

'No, that's not what I said. I told the tale of a goddess who is combing her jet-black hair suspended in eternity.

Back when humanity had not yet been created, tall and beautiful Anahita, the goddess of the sun and love and running water, sat beside the river Ganges, which had not yet been created in India, combing her long hair with a comb made from the tusks of elephants that were yet to be born. The black-eyed goddess grew tired of her wearisome solitude. She wept, creating words and love with which she could compose a poem in praise of her own beauty. Then, in her fertile imagination she saw that love and words and poetry were cold and colourless without human beings. Thus, from her fertile mind she created women and men and enchanting melodies and dances and colours. She saw that human beings needed a place in which to live and time in which to make love. Thus, she created the earth and the sun and the stars and the planets and the mountains and the seas and trees and flowers and rivers and nights and days and living creatures, from whales and camels and horses to birds and butterflies. On the seventh day, she saw that the world looked beautiful in the mirror of her imagination and it was filled with singing and melodies and poetry and colour and love and joy and laughter and dancing. And the indigo and lapis-lazuli butterflies were still alive and the great shah had not yet ordered their mass slaughter so that his dye-makers, mosaic-layers, painters, calligraphers, iconographers and sculptors could steal the rare colours of their wings. Everything was young and transparent and the world spun around the axis of love. Three times three millennia.'

'No. You said that at the end of the third millennium of the seven millennia of the firmaments of antiquity, the male god-dragon, sleeping in the boundless depths of time and the unfathomable darkness of eternity, awakened and bellowed. He looked upon the world that was young and had never known sorrow or longing. He was enraged to see that there was no place for him. No one knew the word for mastery. So the dragon rained down seven millennia of poison and death and decay and vengeance and hatred and power and storms and dirt and desert and drought and sharp daggers onto the world. And, using the litanies he knew, he bound the goddess in chains and sat upon the undisputed throne of mastery. Then, he created interrogators and judges and sermonizers and charlatans and foremen and kings and imams and cables and prisons and torture. And order was established in the world.'

Translated by Nilou Mobasser

Angel Cuadra

The poet Angel Cuadra was born in Havana in 1931. His first collection of poetry was published both in Cuba and abroad. In 1967 he was arrested and accused of having worked against the security of the state. After serving his fifteen-year sentence in full, Cuadra was released in 1982 and three years later emigrated to the USA. A selection of his poetry and essays was published in English translation, under the title *The Poet in Socialist Cuba* in 1994. Cuadra is a member of PEN Cuban Writers in Exile.

The following poems were written in prison in Cuba.

Also at night

Meanwhile the night passes
and silence starts its monotonous drill,
which is the daily round of this idleness
the continuing corrosion of this wrong;
how is it possible that nothing breaks down
that equilibrium continues as a fixed category
like a nail in place –
that life culpably persists
and every day these obscure lives
are being buried metre by metre;
and the wire enclosures,
the symphony of the shackles,
the watchful rifles,

in unpunished collusion
grossly raise asthmatic, sarcastic faces.

Because they are burying, little by little,
these lives which were useful assets
in the total yield of the world.
How can it be that God has less power than this evil,
that hatred is jubilant,
unpunished.
Alas, poor disabled God.

(Written at Melena Dos labour camp, Havana)

The new man

They say to a man,
'Hate this', and he hates it.
They say, 'Seethe with rage and blasphemy',
and he vomits burning spittle of insult
onto the indicated face, which he never saw before.
They say, 'Kill!'
and he plunges the murderous dagger
into the breast ignored until now.
Then he runs off, smiling,
enjoying his portion of blood.
After the horse is broken,
they reward it with pats on the shoulder ...
and he marches, tame and docile
– blind in his vomit –
like a slinking dog.

Afternoon

Rain in sunshine.
Drops of water fall on the grass in the light
as fine as powdered hoarfrost or rain-mist,
and the fields around seem spangled
with blond and gold transparent veils.
The country girl we watch from here – some
with lechery, I almost always, I claim, with tenderness –
finishes work and covers her head;
her mood lightens under this twilight dew
as if she's thinking of a new blouse or a fiesta –
meanwhile a friendly conflict of blues and greys
takes place in the sky.
The livestock move slowly.
Is that the sound of water or singing of birds?
I'm not sure which – confused between the musics.
Further away, like a symbolic circle,
the mountains,
low, but obstinately sure of being mountains.
Somewhere, perplexity appears
with a fixed frown.
Life goes on, low-voiced, crystallized.
And fish pass, absent trees,
other sounds, streets that used to be,
hours falling like sand,
people, smiles, all that is other –
but like phantoms, like footfalls from within.
And then you come back.
The same countryside and damp grass
accepting the afternoon as its destiny.
It is coming back without having moved.
All of this briefly appears through the bars: it is prison.

Meanwhile, twilight falls on the pasture
and a distant bird is not there.

(Guanajay Prison, Havana, Cuba)

Translated by Ruth Fainlight

Yury Bandazhevsky

Born in January 1956 near Grodno, western Belarus, Yury Bandazhevsky was Professor of Pathological Anatomy and Rector of the Gomel Medical Institute when he was arrested in July 1999, on charges of taking bribes from his students and falsifying travel documents in an attempt to escape trial. On 18 June 2001 he was sentenced to eight years in prison. Bandazhevsky's defence is that he did not receive bribes, and that the criminal charges were levied in retaliation for his medical work, highly critical of the government's handling of the after-effects of the nuclear disaster at Chernobyl in 1986. He admitted falsifying documents, but claimed that he did so fearing imprisonment. In prison his health deteriorated significantly, although he continued writing and publishing on the effects of radioactive fallout on the health of the local population. Bandazhevsky was elected an honorary member of various PEN centres and in November/December 2003 there was an international PEN campaign on Bandazhevsky's behalf. On 2 August 2005 he was unexpectedly and conditionally released by President Lukashenko.

In The Philosophy of My Life *(2005) Yury Bandazhevsky tells his story.*

The philosophy of my life

My arrest took place suddenly. On the evening of 13 July 1999, I was in the apartment where I lived with my family. Armed men burst in and began searching the place, destroying everything in their path. Later that evening, when my elder daughter Olga returned home, she was terrified at the sight. My wife and my younger daughter Natalia were in the country. [*The day before, Vladimir Ravkov, the head of the educational department, had also been arrested, and under interrogation had accused Bandazhevsky of taking bribes from the parents of would-be medical students. Later, Ravkov withdrew his allegation, but it served as the pretext for Bandazhevsky's arrest.*]

After searching my offices, and finding nothing illegal there, still less money, the men from the Office against Organized Crime put me into provisional detention, in solitary confinement, having declared that they were arresting me for thirty days under Decree No. 21 of the President of the Republic of Belarus, 'Under urgent measures in the struggle against terrorism and other particularly violent and dangerous crimes.' During the whole of the period following my arrest, they tried to find compromising proofs, and made announcements to this effect in the press, but they were never able to find any proof of my guilt. ... Nothing confirmed their deceitful allegations. Nevertheless, they were sufficient, twenty-five days after my arrest, to find me guilty.

I should also say that a few hours before my arrest, I had in my hands a denunciation signed by Sokolovsk, spokesman for scientific work, addressed to the secretary of the Security Council, Victor Vladimirovitch Cheiman, in which he accused me of all the sins of the world. The most important phrase was that alleging that I was preparing a coup d'état to overthrow the existing government, and that I was receiving funds for this purpose ... This is a total illusion. I have never been interested in politics; my life's work is to study the pathological processes that appear in the human organism under the influence of external environmental factors.

The nervous stress I suffered during the first months of my imprisonment inevitably affected my health. Held in solitary confinement in Moguilev detention centre, where I was taken directly after the charge against me was announced, in defiance of all the rules of common law, I fell ill: utter exhaustion, nausea, stomach pains. The guards took their time before deciding to do anything, but ultimately my state of health became critical, and they took me to the Moguilev clinic. I underwent gastro-intestinal tests, and the doctors discovered a duodenal ulcer. Since the day of my arrest (around a month) I had lost around twenty kilos, and I could hardly move. I only remember the moment when, barely alive, I was laid on a bed, white as snow, and put into handcuffs. I was in a state of total depression almost 24/24. I had no strength to respond to external attacks, although for the most part I felt them. The doctors in that hospital (most of whom I had myself trained) felt compassion for me and tried to help me as much as they could. Slowly, my health improved. I was able to clean my filthy body, more or less – I hadn't been able to wash myself for nearly a month. But a month after I went into hospital, the police came to take me to the Republic's prison hospital at Minsk. [*Bandazhevsky was moved again to another prison in the provinces.*]

There, I suffered until 27 December … I have no wish to deliberately recount the details of the torments I have undergone. I have written this book with the intention of expressing the scientific views which I developed during this period, and which have saved me from decline and despair. That's why, dear reader, I want to talk to you principally about science.

In spite of the brutal and tragic change in my circumstances, and in my social standing, I have never lost the desire to think, reflect and analyse … That affords one immense pleasure, and as long as your strength lasts, you float on a cloud of joy. But when your strength fails, you enter into a state of total devastation, mental and physical, when you don't even have the strength to move.

[*A few months after Bandazhevsky's arrest, the Chair of Pathology at the Gomel Medical Institute was abolished, and his unique collection of embryos presenting with congenital malformation since Chernobyl was destroyed. Meanwhile, released on remand while the case against him was prepared, he worked feverishly to prove the connection between radioactive fallout and malformation in the embryo, carrying out experiments on laboratory animals, the results of which stunned him.*]

We were able to demonstrate that relatively small doses of radio-Caesium induced congenital defects. I believe that this was one of the most successful results in the whole of my long life in scientific research.

[*On 10 June 2001, two days before the verdict on Bandazhevsky was due to be announced, he was allegedly seized in a Minsk street by the KGB and driven towards the Ukrainian border. He believed that he was about to be murdered. But at the border checkpoint, where the KGB agents presented false passports, claiming to be Ukrainian MPs, the scientist shouted at the guards, 'I'm Professor Yury Bandazhevsky. Please help me!' The guards refused to allow the car through. 'You should be grateful to those guards,' Bandazhevsky told his wife, Galina. 'They saved my life.'*

Bandazhevsky was brought to the court in handcuffs and falsely accused of trying to flee the country. On 18 June the judge sentenced him to eight years in prison, without appeal. He was judged by a military tribunal, in breach of international standards of fair trial, and incarcerated in Minsk prison, where he spent the next three years. He had already spent six months in detention on remand. His health continued to deteriorate, and he was hospitalized three times before being operated on for peritonitis.]

Prison Journal, 26 October 2001, 11 o'clock, Friday

I suffer terribly waiting for my lawyer ... because it's impossible for me to prove my innocence. It's hard. I'm cold, and have no comforts of any kind. Am I going to leave this life? And afterwards, what comes afterwards?

Hurt and humiliated, I am imprisoned, and sometimes (quite often) I no longer have faith in the future. These people have no need of my science.

17 July 2002

The heat is unbelievable this summer. It's oppressive. The second hour of the day has passed. Since early this morning, I've been in torment, thinking about the meaning of life: what path has Almighty God prepared for us?

Yes, truly he offers us many paths, and we follow them from earliest infancy. Our parents should help us to choose, to orientate us, but we walk alone. I was born into a family which respected honest, hard work ... When I was very little, I had a good voice ... My music teachers (singing and piano) begged my parents to 'give' me to a musical education. But my father considered the profession of musician with a great degree of scepticism ... He directed me towards a medical milieu ...

That's how it is, God gives a talent which shows itself in a beautiful voice, a sense of musicality, a tendency to write. It would be easy to believe that this is the path he proposes. I chose, not without spiritual torment, another path, that of medical science. I have the impression that somehow the soul of man receives an energy which can guarantee his path in life, and even though he walks an arduous, stony road, this energy will help him reach his goal. That's why it doesn't matter much which path man chooses; he will follow it as much as the

Spiritual Force, invested in him since childhood, permits. He may even be able to magnify it, thanks to his faith in God.

20 July

The accident at the Chernobyl nuclear power station is a catastrophe which no one has been able to hide. (And in this resides its huge importance for the future of humanity.) Nuclear power is a suicidal path for the development of humanity.

In order to survive, we must eliminate nuclear power.

9 October 2003

Today is the birthday of my daughter Natalia, and I dedicate these notes to her.

On 1 October I was operated on for purulent appendicitis.

On 8 October my elder daughter Olga gave birth to a daughter, and they've called her Katia.

At the present time the biosphere is heavily polluted by the products of human activity ... Humanity has learnt the secrets of atomic power ... If one takes into account the fact that during the twentieth century nuclear weapons tests have been badly controlled, and knowing that the security of nuclear reactors is far from perfect, one can say that an enormous quantity of radioactive elements have been released in the biosphere. Humanity, in a wild desire to use scientific knowledge, not only to progress, but also to satisfy base passions, to dominate and conquer ... has created its own sword of Damocles. And if it doesn't raise awareness of what it's done, it's going to die ... Man has become a threat to his own survival.

16 November

Over the last few days, I've been reflecting on my life ... with God's grace, I've managed to consider my knowledge and experience of life in a completely different light. There's no doubt that in other circumstances I wouldn't have been able to do it. If I analyse my career in science, I realize that all its stages haven't happened by chance ... We always think that we create, that we choose our own destiny, our life. But in fact, everything follows the will of God ... The only way of alleviating our fate is to receive the love of God which surrounds us ... but faith in God Almighty does not replace human activity, nor release man from his battle for existence; it only relieves moral suffering and gives the power for this struggle.

27 December

Today I have felt death's icy breath. I don't like writing about my feelings (I even scorn this activity), but now I must note the date; afterwards, I may find myself in another dimension. I feel that my strength is weakening, that something dreadful could happen. I don't know, I don't even want to know what dark, evil forces persecute me. Thank God, I have succeeded in facing up to them, I haven't been tempted to drown in their arms, believing that man, receiving energy from Almighty God, makes his own destiny, and that it's not worth putting your trust in anyone. God makes you strong. Walk on!

[*In January 2005 the Writers in Prison Committee of English PEN organized a petition calling for Bandazhevsky's release. Over 400 British writers signed. Although barred by the government from visiting Professor Bandazhevsky in his settlement, English PEN delegates were able to speak to him by telephone. He told us that his 'PEN library', books sent by members, reminded him that, as an Honorary Member, he was part of an international community of writers who were working for his release.]*

Translated from the French by Carole Seymour-Jones

Koigi wa Wamwere

Koigi wa Wamwere, a writer, human rights activist and MP, was arrested on 18 September 1993 in Kenya. He was charged with possession of weapons and seditious publications (copies of documents from the National Democratic Human Rights Organization led by Wa Wamwere). He was also charged with illegally entering a restricted security zone where ethnic clashes were reported to be taking place. The writer had been under surveillance, since treason charges against him were dropped, and had been detained on two other occasions.

Wa Wamwere was released on bail, but was rearrested on 5 November and accused of being linked to a raid on Bahati police station. He was charged with attempted robbery of guns with violence and possession of arms without a certificate. There were numerous irregularities concerning his trial, and the charges followed a pattern of harassment against human rights activists, opposition figures and journalists who, like wa Wamwere, were attempting to investigate or report incidents of political violence in the Rift Valley and other parts of Kenya. Wa Wamwere was finally released in 1996 on medical grounds.

The following extract is taken from wa Wamwere's book Conscience on Trial, *published by Africa World Press Inc. in 1983*

If I tell you where I am sick
You ask prison officers

'Is that so?'
You treat me to satisfy prison officers
And not to cure my disease.
You consult police and prison officers
Before you prescribe me anything.

Prison doctors,
You recommend that poor food
Is wholesome for me.
You recommend that my health is all right
with a sisal mat and two worn out dirty blankets for my
     beddings
You recommend me fit for hard labor
When I am so sick that I am on the verge of death
You refuse to recommend for me good food
When my ailing health desperately needs it
You shut your eyes to
Disease-causing prison conditions
And pretend to be an enemy of diseases
That are born out of those very conditions.

You free prison authorities from blame
When they murder me with their brutality
You recommend that I am fit
To be given sterilizing strokes
You recommend that I am fit
To be hanged
You have become servants of death.

Prison doctors,
Your spotlessly white robes
Deceive us
They make you look clean

But in your service of death and oppression
You 'are like unto whited sepulchres
Which indeed appear beautiful outward
But are within full of dead men's bones
And of all uncleanliness.'

Doctors,
Serve life
Fight death
Unchain prisoners' and detainees' health
From the shackles of prison oppression
Don't be in prison to imprison life
Be in prison to give free rein to life
Be in prison to alleviate suffering and oppression
And not increase and excuse them.
If you let prisoners see liberators
If you let prisoners see
The antitheses of prison guards and officers
In you let prisoners see hope and life.

Chris Abani

Chris Abani was a political prisoner in Nigeria between 1985 and 1991. Following the publication of his novel *Masters of the Board,* he was arrested in 1985, as his work was considered a blueprint for the foiled coup of General Vatsa. He was detained initially for six months in two three-month stretches. In 1987 Abani joined a university guerrilla theatre group, which performed plays in front of public buildings and government offices. He was rearrested and held in the notorious Kiri Kiri maximum security prison. He was released without charge or explanation and returned to his university studies. His play *Song of a Broken Flute,* written for the 1990 convocation ceremony for the university, led to his final period of incarceration for eighteen months. He spent six months in solitary confinement. Abani was sentenced to death for treason – without trial – and held on death row. English PEN helped with his rehabilitation in the UK following his final release.

Chris's poems provide a harrowing description of his prison experiences and the torture he suffered. They were first published in a collection entitled Kalakuta Republic, *published by Saqi Books in 2000.*

Portal

I.
When first arrested
18.
Excited by possibilities of fame;
inflamed by
legends of political prisoners: sure that
Amnesty would free me.

But the days
dragged
into months;
no charge
no sign
of camera-toting journalists
from Reuters;
no word
from my family
no amnesty.

Caught in the cross-hairs of fear,
the only way to mark
the days is by counting the beatings
3 a day
62 days: 186.

Housed in comfort; relative to;
I watch the trials on TV of
my co-conspirators; stomach fisted
waiting
my turn.
But they are too embarrassed to try me.

6 months later
unable to hold me any longer and
no doubt alarmed
at how much it
costs
to feed me; they give in
I am free to go

II.
1987,
deciding to take them on
I
stand
daily; reciting their crimes in epics
daring them: 'Go on. Kill me. Make me famous.'

They do
But 20 is not 18
Guns, boots, truncheons, knuckles
I realise – too late –
this time it's for real
I've had my dress rehearsal.

Pain draws out time razor sharp
but I am unbeaten;
I martyr my anger
profaning their idolatrous power
again;
straight to jail; I do not pass go

Shovelling
with three fingers cold corn porridge
into my mouth,

the enormity of it:
I am being held by killers
and nobody knows I am here.

Kiri Kiri
Maximum Security prison
D wing; or E, I forget
With the worst of the head cases:
Fela Anikulapo Kuti
Smiling: 'Truth, my young friend, is a risky business.'

Passion Fruit

Here

Sex is not always a choice
lovingly made and enjoyed like
plump well-handled self-chosen fruit
teeth sinking into soft flesh in a dribble of pleasure.

Nevertheless
it abounds.

Some because it is the
truth of their being.

Some to deny, negate, sate
deep yearning, wordless, timeless.

Even the most rabid homophobe
can give in
to gentle caresses

comfort in this loveless, concrete
cesspit.

Some never do
and not from fear and loathing.

Some erupt in
painful, bloody, self-annihilating rape.

Some fall in
love; soft green moss caressing crumbling walls.

Some, unable to stomach
the truth that all love is light,
amputate their own penes, laughing insanely
as they bleed to a stump.

Concrete Memories

In an empty cell,
stone
worn
tortured
scalded
by tides
of warm blood
and water,
petrifies their guilt.

Nicknamed
Kalakuta Republic
in some distant pain

by inmate or guard.
Techniques to extract confessions:
tried, tested, proven.
Interrogations are carried out.

Teeth,
pulled from their roots
with rusty pliers.
Methodical, clinical; each
raw tender wound
disinfected by gentle cigarette embers
and rubbing alcohol
mixed with salt for extra bite.

Rusty
cold
barrel of Winchester
bolt-action Mark IV rifle;
retired right
arm of imperialism.
Enema. Rammed
up rectum, repeatedly;
twirling cocktail
swizzle-stick.
Extremely effective, they say
at dislodging caked-in conspiracies.

The Box

Wooden frame with skirt of sheet metal
6 foot by 3 foot by 3 foot.

Pin-pricks of air burn holes on the negative
of my body; choking on my own smell mingled
with scent of seared hair and skin,
I taste my pungent mortality.

One hour later:

Religion unfurls in desperate splendour.
Silently through old man's mumbling lips
prayers tumble forth; spells to keep the
terror at bay; currency to buy salvation.

Matthew, Mark, Luke and John,
bless this bed that I lie on.
Before I lay my head to sleep
I beg thee, Lord, my soul to keep.

Two hours later:

Fear cramps me into panic; hysterical
I beat frantically, futilely at the sides.
2 inches is inadequate leeway; I only
brand dull thumps onto taut knuckles.

Three hours later:

Counting out time on beads of sweat
to keep from going insane. Mental
arithmetic. 2678 divide by the pi of 7.
Nursery rhymes work also – except when tears
muffle memory.

Four hours later:

Blank face, blank black eyes stare; icy
dense darkness; free falling, nothing below
except inky space sucking me into maw.
These are some of my nameless terrors.
Five hours later:

Water is thrown over the metal to cool me.
Through burning steam I see
a man in dazzling robes; face, a thousand suns
coming towards me; leading to light …

Six hours later:

'… Jesu, Jesu, Jesu …'
chants bubble through blisters.
'Poor devil', someone in the cell mutters
'Shut up fool!' another snarls.

Someone else, too impatient
to reach the hole in the floor
stands arms akimbo
spattering my face with urine.

'Thank you, thank you …' I mumble
as the hot ammonia stings me

into life.

José Revueltas

José Revueltas was born in Durango, Mexico, in 1914. He was imprisoned on a number of occasions for his work for the Communist Party and other left-wing organizations. His first incarceration inspired *Los muros de agua* (*The Walls of Water*), a novel about the Islas Marías, two islands used as prisons. In 1968 he was detained for his support of the student movement for civil freedoms. He was finally released but died in 1976 shortly after the authorities ordered his return to prison.

The following is an edited version of a letter Reveueltas wrote to Arthur Miller during his incarceration at 'the black palace of Lecumberri'. Miller responded to Revuletas and sent appeals on his behalf.

To Señor Arthur Miller, President of International PEN

Dear Arthur Miller,

[…] Shortly after 8 p.m. on 1 January 1970, from inside our cells along corridor M in the Lecumberri Preventative Penitentiary, we heard the voice of a comrade calling out from his corridor, telling us in alarmed tones that all the visitors who had come into corridor M that afternoon had been detained for over two hours, without being allowed to leave the jail and go into the city. In fact, our visitors had left shortly after six in the evening, and we'd naturally assumed they were well on their way home from the prison, so a deep sense of disquiet overcame those who had only most recently bade their relatives farewell. At the sound of this alarm call [we] left our cells for the small interior garden at the end of the corridor, to gather behind the railings separating our garden from a heavy door made of double iron sheets, which in turn gives onto the circular corridor (one we call the 'circus' for its similarity to the 'arena' of a bull ring) in the centre of which stands the watchtower known as 'the polygon'.

A group of some twenty of us gathered at the doorway to corridor M in order to ask the cell guard what had happened to our relatives, and to allow delegates – or even a single delegate – through to obtain trustworthy information regarding them. The guards drily rejected our request, moving away from the door with an air of distracted vagueness and indifference, to disappear around the other side of the 'circus'. An unusually empty and desolate jail appeared before our eyes, without a single guard or any other representative to appeal to. A strange and oppressive feeling pervaded the place. Then, from a distance, women's and children's voices, a muffled yelling, began to reach our ears. 'Political prisoners! Political prisoners!' they chorused. It was impossible to resist a call like that. We banged frantically on the doors, some ran round the other side and seized a barbell from the gym room to break the chains. The bolts gave way and we were out in the 'circus'.

We ran towards the shouting. There they were in a corridor, imprisoned behind a tall barred door – women, men and children, our relatives and visitors. (Not my wife, however; by chance she had left an hour before the close of visiting time that day.) There was nothing at all we could do, since our intention was simply to talk to the prison director, or with his deputy, responsible for matters of surveillance. The former's name is General Andres Puentes Vargas and the latter's, Major Bernardo Palacios. But there was nobody in charge of the jail at the time or, to put it another way, General Puentes Vargas and Major

Palacios, who were indeed there, had taken on a very different kind of authority that afternoon. They were at the head of the well-fed and compressed lines of about a hundred common-law prisoners who constituted an 'elite', commissioned to undertake the most diverse administrative functions inside the prison: as 'majors' and 'officers' of the corridors; 'clerks', 'gofers', 'messengers', 'errand boys', each one of their unusual offices had its own boss, meaning, of course, the most feared ruffian amongst them. The prison director and his deputy, on this occasion, decided to pursue the dubious honour of authorizing gangs of the worst evil-doers, from those with the blackest reputations.

Those of us who had exited from Corridor M paused some fifty metres from the point where we came face to face with a tight mass of the 'conscripts', together with the General and the Major, standing close at hand ... between us a no-man's-land, a barred passageway where the visitors found themselves trapped. All that followed happened with a dreamlike, phantasmagoric rapidity. A troop of comrades from corridor C came up behind us, a group of students who initially caused us surprise for appearing so very young. At the same moment, the criminals from corridor D – who had had their doors opened – advanced on the tumult, now armed with metal pipes, iron bars and clubs ... Projectiles were raining on us from every side, including bottles, stones and partition walls, in the midst of the noise of windows shattering into shards, and shouts, yells, swearing in voices no one could understand. Before my eyes, and with gestures that seemed to me singularly slow and calm, a screw placed a key in a padlock on corridor E, carefully turned it a couple of times, in the expert manner of a professional, then removed the lock and the door opened in an instant.

For a few seconds, everyone on corridor E vacillated, perplexed, without daring to take those few paces onto the 'circus'. Then all the occupants of corridor E emerged in an avalanche, to join those from D, and threw themselves at us without delay, attacking our rearguard, to squeeze us between the two gangs. In the instamatic flash of a camera shutter I saw the shape of the General, agitatedly waving his arms over his head, with a black object in his right hand. Rapidly, there followed precisely differentiated detonations; the General emptied the entire contents of his pistol into the air.

The result was a rapid-fire round of bullets that seemed to erupt from every imaginable corner, above and below, in front and behind, and from every side. The screws from 'the big wall' and 'the polygon' started firing in turn. 'Take refuge in corridor M, into M!' we all yelled. This had to be the only place – we thought – where we could find sanctuary ... There we dispersed, furious with frustration and impotence, but also reluctant to do battle with common prisoners. If we did – of this we were certain – it would be to respond to a monstrous provocation plotted by the government to do us down. Now, when it was the least of our intentions, we had finally fallen into their trap.

Inside corridor M, there was no time to close the doors. A group of comrades decided we should lock ourselves in cell number 21, which seemed the most secure, and where we might prevent our assailants from entering, assuming we were able to barricade ourselves in adequately. Behind the door of cell 21, we stacked a table, some beds, and any other pieces of furniture we could, then shot the bolt on the door. Within minutes, the sack of the corridor began, followed by the siege of our cell. 'At them! Get at them!' was the war cry, inciting others to throw themselves on their victims with maximum force and speed, making the most of a propitious moment when we were least able to defend ourselves or make a protest.

At this point it becomes unnecessary to continue any further with this account. They beat us; stripped us of all we had – pens, watches, etc.; they sacked our cells without leaving behind a single one of our belongings, including our desks, typewriters, books, beds, mattresses, clothes, manuscripts, the lot. Books and books. What possible use could Hegel's *Phenomenology*, Lukács's *Aesthetics*, Marx's *1844 Manuscripts*, or Proust's *Correspondence* with his mother be to these miserable looters? As regards the outcome of my originals, I struck lucky. My cell floor was covered with a carpet of untidy papers, stapled according to themes and content, and I managed to salvage most of them. I lost a cardboard box containing some fifteen folders filled with inessential papers, and I no longer possess a typewriter on which to type up a clean version of my scripts, since I always first write them out by hand. De Gortari, a doctor of philosophy, disgracefully ended up losing his irreplaceable originals, in which he'd invested whole years of work. He clasped me, moaning with pain, when we met up inside his devastated cell.

When at long last the criminals allowed us out of cell 21, having showered blows and punches all over our bodies, the corridor was still filled with villains, coming and going with looted articles. What was truly incomprehensible was that there, among them, the guardians of our penal system were walking from one end of the corridor to the other in an indifferent and tranquil manner, swinging their truncheons round and round their wrists, as if they had simply come across one another on some unassuming afternoon's walk. What were they doing there, if not protecting the victims of an attack? Very simply, they were directing the activities of the criminals, showing them the doors off the relevant corridors where they could leave unseen, taking their booty with them. I can still remember the expression the screw used as we crossed in the doorway to cell 21. Gazing at me with a smile on his face, he said, 'Are you hurt, Maestro?' before answering himself with, 'Just a few little blows, weren't they?' No, I wasn't hurt. Just a rain of punches to the face, nothing more.

These are the events that took place on New Year's Day, 1970, seen by one who was at the same time witness, participant and victim ...

JOSÉ REVUELTAS

Translated by Amanda Hopkinson

Shi Tao

The journalist and poet Shi Tao was arrested in China on 24 November 2004 for posting online his notes of the government's plans to handle news coverage of the fifteenth anniversary of the Tiananmen Square massacre. These plans had been read out at an editorial meeting of the newspaper *Dangdai Shangbao* (*Contemporary Trade News*) in April 2004. He sent his notes to an overseas website using a Yahoo! email account. According to court documents, Yahoo! (Hong Kong) Holdings Ltd provided the Chinese authorities with Shi Tao's identity. He was sentenced on 30 April 2005 to ten years' imprisonment for 'revealing state secrets to a foreign entity'.

Shi Tao has worked as a freelance journalist for several newspapers and has also written a number of articles, including political commentaries, for online forums, in particular the overseas Chinese website *Min Zhu Lun Tan* (*Democracy Forum*). He has published several books of poetry. At the time of writing the cyber-dissident remains in prison and is said to be suffering from respiratory problems as a result of forced labour.

The following are two of his poems.

June

My whole life
Will never get past 'June'

June, when my heart died
When my poetry died
When my lover
Died in an abandoned pool of blood

June, the scorching sun burns open my skin
Revealing the true nature of my wound
June, the fish swims out of the blood-red sea
Towards another place to hibernate
June, the earth shifts, the rivers fall silent
Piled-up letters unable to be delivered to the dead

Translated by Chip Rolley

Pain

The portrait on the wall has lost its powers of
     reflection,
yet the wind at my window cannot stem this violence.
I torment you through one long night of passion
till we're both completely spent – two kites left in the
     rain.

Once, long ago, I was the star of a children's play.
Once, long ago, I used both my hands to teach children
     to sing.
Once, long ago, I heard two crows conversing, lit by the
     moon.

But the brute fact of cruelty
struck me down. Pain lacks the tenderness of
     moonlight.

Struggling, trapped in an iron box full of lies, I try to be
  a model patient,
to swallow a spoonful of spite down the throat of the
  motherland.

Translated by Sarah Maguire and Heather Inwood

Sihem Ben Sedrine

Sihem Ben Sedrine has suffered persecution for her writing and editing in Tunisia over many years. She is the founder and editor of the online magazine *Kalima* and the spokesperson for the National Freedom Council (Conseil National des Libertés) in Tunisia. PEN mounted an international campaign on her behalf to commemorate International Women's Day in 2005.

The following letter was written by Sihem Ben Sedrine during a brief stint in prison in Tunisia, on 28 July 2001.

Dear friends,

For one month I have shared my fate with twenty-four prisoners in a room measuring 10 x 4 metres, whose heavy doors are closed with great uproar by the guards in order to emphasize our imprisonment.

Every morning that God provides, the sound of heavy copper keys clanking together warns us that in thirty minutes it is time for the roll call. They count us again, like well-guarded cattle. This is repeated four times every day and we have to use all our imagination in order to fill the time that never seems to end ... The young girls who make up three quarters of the barracks let their *joie de vivre* burst out when the sound of music emanates from our insipid national television. But sorrow catches up with them; disputes arise, punctuated by lamentations about their broken lives.

There is refuge in illness and it takes all the art of a great drama to make the guard in charge of the pharmacy give us the miracle cure, aspirin. It almost takes a riot and the beating down of doors in cases of extreme urgency. They are taken to hospital in handcuffs and wrapped in *safsaris* after being body-searched. Undressed, you are reduced to an object, hands insulting the most intimate parts of your body, under a rhythmic string of lewd words – 'whores' – 'bend down' – 'cough'.

Dear friends, contrary to rumour I do not like it in prison and I can't wait to leave, despite the cachet it seems to provide me. I have faced it because for me exile is worse, and I salute those who have the courage to endure it.

I knew that my fate was sealed and that, for those in control, the spirit of revenge is stronger than the reason of the state. The only thing left me was the satisfaction of having expressed myself freely.

Dear friends, I am deeply moved by the solidarity that you have shown me. The fact that my freedom matters so much to you is the best gift I have ever received.

Translated from the French by Cecilie Torjussen

Javier Tuanama Valera

The Peruvian Javier Tuanama Valera, the former editor-in-chief of *Hechos* magazine, was first detained in October 1990, accused of belonging to the terrorist group Movimiento Revolucionario Tupac Amaru (MRTA). After more than three years in prison he was absolved of these charges in March 1994 and released. However, he was immediately rearrested on new charges of collaborating with MRTA and in connection with other terrorism cases. The allegations against Tuanama Valera were made by a confessed terrorist who says that he met the journalist in December 1990 to discuss terrorist activities. Tuanama Valera was in prison at this time many miles from where he was alleged to have met his accuser. Human rights groups believed that Tuanama Valera's accuser made the allegations in the hope of securing a more lenient penalty for himself under repentance laws. The journalist was finally released on 16 November 2002, under the terms of a pardon extended by the Peruvian president, Alejandro Toledo.

The following poem was written in prison and is dated 5 February 1994.

Silent impatience

How difficult it is to live with the suffering
of an uncertain and overcast world.
How difficult, when our values

are ripped to pieces under a dark shadow;
and behind its cloak, indifference
becomes a silent impatience
which draws out the hours
like in sleepless nights.
If only the weight of its rule would cease
bearing down on these bitter hours!

How long will the price of this foolish hatred
be paid by those
who seek justice and mercy
with the truth?
How long will hypocrisy
overlook pleading hands
while people are suffering
in pain and crying out?

If only the echoes of my voice
could be heard from these confines
and people could know that the results
of this terrible crime will not remain unpunished.

But the days pass
and times change
like the seasons
where not all are cold
not all are bitter
where some bring success and happy emotions.

An old saying goes that
when the river sings out
it is because it is carrying stones.
The meaning, if you look for it

and decipher the omen,
is that something is finishing
and a new beginning will come
full of surprise and hope
where intrigue and sadness
will soon be banished.

Grigory Pasko

Grigory Pasko is a journalist and poet who worked for the Russian Navy's newspaper *Boyevaya Vakhta* and also as a freelance journalist for the Japanese media. After reporting on Russia dumping nuclear waste into the sea, Pasko was arrested in 1997 for the possession of state secrets with intent to supply them abroad. Initially he was acquitted of treason but charged with abusing his military office.

On 25 December 2001, Pasko was sentenced on appeal to four years' imprisonment. He was found guilty of one of the ten charges of treason brought against him – notes Pasko had taken as a journalist present at a meeting of the Pacific Fleet were deemed to contain classified information. From the time of Pasko's arrest, PEN and other human rights organizations questioned the legitimacy of proceedings against him, and raised concerns that he was being prosecuted in violation of his right to free expression, and as a punishment for reporting on an issue that was in the public interest.

Pasko was released on 23 January 2003, when a civilian court overruled the previous decisions made by military courts. He remains in Russia, where he edits and writes for the magazine *Environment and Rights*.

The following are some of his poems.

Tomorrow I'm flying off to the war

Tomorrow I'm flying off to the war.
Perhaps I'll regret that I got involved,
perhaps later someone will find me
guilty of not refusing.

Tomorrow I'm flying off to the war.
I am a journalist and that means that I must,
for my own sake, lift the shroud
of confusion, not staining it with lies.

Tomorrow I'm flying off to the war:
to find out who are ours and who not ours.
I shall remember the dead with bitter vodka
and will look into the eyes of those who haven't fallen
    yet.

I don't want to sit it out in a shaky silence.
I know: without me they won't write everything.
In hot Grozny the dirty snow melts
from the hoarse screams of wounded mates.

Tomorrow I'm flying off … And on the way
I'll think often about this bloody massacre …
Perhaps it would be simpler to find
coffins for those who started this war.

In my prison

In my prison
my cries can't reach God,
but each time

I pray: 'Don't forget' …
If I were free
I wouldn't need
much in this life.
The road as well
so I could go
down it to somewhere,
so that the stars,
slowly burning,
could stream down
into my palms
like morning dew.

In my prison
it's already my second autumn
which with carefree
dispassion scatters
the leaves of the calendar
into the New Year.

Quietly I return into the childhood

Quietly I return into the childhood
by the stars of the constellations,
where the weight of worries
and illnesses is insignificant,
where the ragged storms
shouted rain
over the vineyards
and under the slate of the houses,
where the song flows smoothly
in the night among the leaves:

suddenly the cricket burbled out
like a silvery spring.
I need to go somewhere,
to be lost in it:
in that land, which we call
with quiet sadness, childhood.

Translated by Richard McKane

Andrej Dynko

Andrej Dynko is the vice-editor-in-chief of the Belarusian independent newspaper *Nasha Niva*, editor of the cultural magazine *Arche*, a writer and translator, and vice-president of the Belarus PEN Centre. He was arrested on 21 March 2006 on his way to October Square in Minsk, reportedly to provide food and support to demonstrators who had camped there in protest against the national elections.

Dynko was apprehended on a bus by two plain-clothes police and subsequently charged with 'hooliganism', for using 'bad language'. He was given a ten-day sentence. Shortly before the elections, Dynko was quoted in *Le Monde diplomatique*: 'Lukashenka's regime could turn out to be a historic opportunity for Belarus finally to come together as a nation, in opposition to this regime built on lies and hollow state ideology.' He was released on 1 April 2006.

The following is an edited version of a letter he wrote from prison in Minsk, It first appeared in Nasha Niva *weekly.*

Sacrificial therapy
Letter from a prison in Minsk

I am writing these lines on Monday at 11 p.m. The lights are out, but the prison is not sleeping. It is as loud as a jungle in the night. Voices and even laughter can be heard from the cells. The sounds of the prison remind me of a summer camp for children. During the day the prisoners play chess (with figures sculpted from bread), 'mafia' and battleships and solve crossword puzzles. When the night comes, it is time for verbal games. Prisoners recall the riot police and guards they have met, and tell spicy jokes about the dictator and his camarilla, state radio hosts and sergeants who were gathered from all corners of the Belarusian capital to Akrestsina prison in Minsk. 'Calm down, motherf*****!' – the guards remind the prisoners about their existence, but the buzz doesn't get any quieter. There is a light bulb in a small window above the door. It gives me enough light to write.

An hour ago, the guard told the guys in the cell opposite us that 300 more arrested are being taken to Akrestsina. It sounds unreal, it's difficult to believe him. Who can joke like that after a whole week of continuous arrests? We heard of the last big transport of prisoners on Saturday. First there was a rumour that a 15,000-strong protest march was heading towards Akrestsina. Two hours later the interior minister, Navumau, confirmed this in his interview with Belarusian state radio. The prison met his words with chants of 'Long live Belarus!' accompanied by rumbling and clanking at the radiators. Barely warm now, they are totally cold during the day.

We sit in a new prison building, not yet completed but already full of those arrested in the square and around it. There are eight of us in a cell designed for five, and, by using a method of proportion, we try to estimate the number of internees. We have no idea how many cells there are in the old prison building. There are about forty in the new one. How many of us are there? Five hundred? Six hundred? Belarusian state radio, the only means of information we have, doesn't tell us anything about the numbers of the arrested – a clear sign that the number is huge!

The old building is warm, but stinks like a homeless tramp. There are no single beds here. We are proud to receive packages from the outside. Some women have not chosen the most convenient husbands for themselves.

The prison unites. There are a lot of us, and we watch as our optimistic power catches the attention of convoy guards. The novices stare at us, start talking. Some even flash V-signs through the peepholes of our doors – and this is our victory. 'Why so sad, guys?' asks one of them. 'Over there, in the women's cell, there are syringes and porn magazines'. [*Shortly after the tent camp dispersal, Belarusian state television showed the images of the tent camp, allegedly full of drug accessories and pornographic publications.*] We burst into laughter.

We are listening to the radio. We hear about the looming social crisis in France, and that as a result of Irish pubs going bankrupt, 1,200 people have lost their jobs. The victory of Orange forces in the Ukraine becomes clear when we hear that the state radio is reporting the alleged chaos at Ukrainian polling stations. Nine times a day we hear the Belarusian Foreign Ministry wrathfully condemning US and EU interference in Belarusian affairs, and we know: they ask for our release.

Who are my fellow inmates? Mostly people who have been imprisoned for the first time in their lives. Mostly young, eighteen- to thirty-five-year-olds. A computer programmer from Minsk; a DJ from Mahilyou; a sole trader from the Dinamo market in Minsk. There is a businessman in a cashmere coat, who is also a Protestant priest; a worker and musician from Homel; a journalist from the newspaper *Belarusy i Rynok*, Vadzim Alyaksandrovich; and a Minsk plumber, also experienced in translating American cartoons into Belarusian.

Akrestsina cells have a vibrant spiritual life. The preachers preach about ordeals which God sent to Joseph, dissidents with twenty years of experience tell about the deeds of past times. There is no grief, no fear. There is a feeling of a fulfilled duty. 'Who, if not us?' says the manager from Hrodna, who loaded the trunk of his Ford with ham, cheese and tangerines and, at 6 a.m. on 21 March, set off for Minsk. He reached the square, and was arrested there.

I was arrested on the morning of 21 March, after the first night in the square. I was not alone in the police bus – riot police loaded it with people who had heard about the tent camp on the Russian television channel NTV or on the internet. The first reaction was solidarity. I recognised my neighbour. We knew each other's faces, but had never said 'Hi!' to each other before. In 1996, the courts fined people for scuffling with police. In 2006, they sentence young women to seven days on a plank bed without mattresses for [carrying] a flask with tea.

There was no revolution, there was a protest. If there are any reasonable people in power, they cannot help but pay attention to the fact that two out of every three cars passing the square honked as a sign of solidarity with the protesters. People say traffic police reported the numberplates to police blockades further down the road. The drivers were stopped and fined two blocks away from the square. In the square itself, the authorities played the game of 'democratic facade'.

I am sitting on a long wooden bench (where I also sleep). It is twenty-eight centimetres wide – I measured it with a pack of cigarettes. My fellow inmates have their backs pressed against each other on the plank bed. The night is so freezing that they have to sleep reversed, facing each others' toes, bundling up their legs with their coats. The cold crawls inside through the iron-barred hole, where the fire alarm is, which leads into the corridor. The chilly wind drifts through the chinks in the window. Akrestsina is finally quiet. Socks dry on a radiator. Kent cigarette butts stick out of the ashtray made out of bread. The brown wooden floor reflects the light of the bulb, a guard is coughing in the corridor, a small square window holds the feeding-trough, its contents ooze out on the tin-reinforced door. If you don't suffer from claustrophobia, it is quiet and calm here. Everything is provided for you, nothing depends on you.

Being imprisoned feels like being pregnant: it's worrisome in the beginning, and at the end. Prisoners discuss which provocation awaits them at the prison exit. Almost everyone here has an acquaintance who is under politically motivated criminal investigation. It was especially painful to hear from Siarhej S***** that secret services stealthily put drugs into the home of Kastus Shydlouski, the museum conservator from Braslau. One can expect everything from this regime. The worst tricks of Soviet times are back, and the machinery of repression has grown much greater.

The Soviet Union prepared itself for war with the outside enemy and invested in advanced missiles. Lukashenko's regime invests everything in fighting the internal enemy. That is why secret paramilitary units, special departments of the Presidential Security Service, and the KGB have grown bigger and multiplied. Above them is the Security Council with Viktar Lukashenka, the president's son, who is in charge of it all. Internal forces have grown several times larger, in comparison to Soviet times. As far as I can tell from personal contacts, the regime will be able to rely on a thousand handpicked fighters from special troops for as long as it can pay their salaries. Elite units are being trained in the spirit of absolute devotion to the orders of their commander; the law is not important for them …

It is getting light outside, which means that cell number 13 will wake up soon. I have to finish this letter: it is impossible to write when the inmates are talking, smoking or satisfying themselves by your side.

It doesn't matter any more whether you break the law. You can be expelled, fired, beaten up, detained or imprisoned any time you begin any activity which is considered to be in opposition to the regime.

The regime wanted to strangle the tent camp by blockading it, to take it over by starvation. The regime showed its true nature by arresting people who were going to the toilet, by grabbing young women who were carrying Thermoses, and by hiding the *autozaki* – trucks for the transportation of detainees – behind the billboards reading 'For a prosperous Belarus!' For this regime, the television image outweighs everything else. The authorities locked up everybody they saw as potential organizers of protests; then they arrested everybody who seemed to stir up the protests. But the unexpected happened – three new people took the place of each one who had been arrested, and people began to carry food about their bodies. Photographers documented a boy who, happily smiling, undressed and removed the sausages wrapped around his waist.

The existence of the tent camp inspired thousands of people to heroic deeds, both large and small. These deeds will stay with those people for years, lightening their hearts.

Sacrificial therapy – that was the sense of the 2006 protests. The regime understood that it had lost. It clumsily cleared the tent camp. That didn't help, so the authorities staged a truly primitive provocation on Freedom Day, 25 March. This is my vision of those days, most of which I had to spend behind bars. Please forgive me if I am wrong. I am among people who have undergone sacrificial therapy, and these are bright days among bright people.

27 March, 11 p.m.–28 March, 6 a.m.

Translated by Ales Kudrycki

Thich Tue Sy

The Vietnamese scholar, philosopher and writer the Venerable Thich Tue Sy (lay name Pham Van Thuong) was arrested along with eleven other Buddhist monks and nuns in March 1984, accused of membership of the illegal organization the National Front for Human Rights. Thich Tue Sy was sentenced to death in 1988 but his sentence was later commuted to twenty years imprisonment. As a professor at the Van Hanh university in the 1970s he was one of the most authoritative voices on Nagajuna philosophy. He was released from prison in 1998.

The following are four of his poems written in prison.

Stone walls

My stone walls are adorned with valueless decor.
No sunset would penetrate this cage.
A lonely man stares at a flickering lamp;
All history's words cannot describe these
heartfelt emotions.

Early bathing

Rising early to bathe
I stand relaxed
With immortal disposition
No water could purify further.

Narrow cell

Here in my narrow cell I am free.
Stolling leisurely,
I talk, laugh with myself,
cast a longing eye towards the eternal Sun.

Goodbye to Prison

Goodbye to prison
I live emptily in this world:
Within borderless realms I study Zen
Nothing, no one
Nothing to do but watch the flowers strewn amid the
    heavens.

Translated by Trevor Carolan and Frederick Young

Hwang Dae-Kwon

Born in 1956, Hwang Dae-Kwon (Bau) was arrested in June 1985 at Kimpo International airport in Seoul, South Korea, upon his return from a holiday in the United States, where he was studying political science. He was accused of writing articles for an overseas Korean newspaper, *Haeuim-inbo*, which were critical of his government and the United States. He was also accused of meeting North Korean agents while in the USA, and was linked to an espionage group by his government. He was originally sentenced to life imprisonment, later reduced to twenty years. He was seriously tortured within the first sixty days of his detention, when he was forced to 'confess' to the charges of espionage. PEN members remained in contact with Bau through much of his time in prison. He was finally released in 1998, under amnesty, and came to the UK to study at agricultural college in 2000.

Bau wrote to his sister about the small garden he tended while in prison, and included musings on his prison life. In 2002 the letters, spanning a period of over six years and three prisons, were made into a book, *The Wildflower Letters*, which became a bestseller in Korea.

The following are edited extracts from letters and emails to his PEN friends tell a small part of Hwang's story. Bau is his Catholic name.

25-11-92

Dear Mr. Pauline Neville,

I have received the book you sent with great pleasure. Thank you so much. The fact that someone on the opposite side of the globe thinks of me encourages me not to fall into forced pessimism which is derived from the long solitary confinement. Yes, I'm hungry for news from the outer world, especially news from personal experience. Here I have only two information about you: your name and the book, *Caligula*. I imagine about you based upon these information; maybe you are a man, aged in your fifties's and a writer? Why the book *Caligula*? Is he interesting or just a present to an Asian friend?

Let me introduce myself to you. I'm thirty-seven-years-old now, seven and a half years have passed since my arrest. Originally sentenced [to] life long imprisonment, but [it] was [commuted] to twenty years, three years ago. A graduate student of political science at the time of being arrested. Most of all, I'm not the spy they accused me of. This is my very short personal history.

Dear Mr. Neville. I'm passing my eighth winter in the prison. I hope that this winter will not be hard for me because of your warm encouragement. Ah! I missed one thing. Although my dream to be a professor was broken, I have been studying hard on my major that is on third world development, dreaming I could someday contribute myself to the people of the third world.

Looking forward to your reply.
God bless you.
Sincerely yours,
Audong Korea,
Hwang

14 July 1993

Dear Christa,

I received three letters from you and a wonderful birthday present. (my birthday is 17th July). I really don't know how to thank you for all your kindness.

I wrote you on 2 June but you didn't say anything about my letter in your recent letter. It must have gone missing. After all this comes to be the first letter to you. I have to introduce myself once again.

You said you are a widow. Likewise I am a widower too but much younger than you. At the time I was imprisoned nine years ago, I had a lovely wife and a baby (son). But severe environment around her and my very long prison-term made her divorce me. She could not manage her life as a wife of a 'SPY' in this hysterically anti-communist country. It goes without saying that the title 'SPY' was fabricated for the political purpose. Since separation she took the baby and I know nothing of them. All I can do at this time is pray for them.

I am thirty-eight-years-old, a CATHOLIC, and was a graduate student of political science before being imprisoned. My hobby is similar to you. Love all kind of music, literature, flowers (especially wild flowers), trees, outdoor life, sports and watching movies. In here, I usually play tennis in exercise time.

Your picture-letter is very interesting. You could show me all the flowers in your garden in that way. Whenever you send the flower picture, please write down the name of it. I have my flower garden here. It's composed of wild flowers. Some are raised only for watching, others are only for eating. This small garden is my sole comfort.

Dear Christa, I'm very glad to come to know you, and thanks very much for your warm encouragement. I'd like to know more about you and your family. I wish you good health and peace in your mind. God bless you!

Yours sincerely,

from Audong, Korea

Hwang

P.S. Don't forget numbering your letter.

24 August 1994

Dear Christa,

Thank you for your letters of August. How much I thank you for your warm affection! And beautiful photos too. The flat you live in looks very nice. Do you live on 3rd floor? I wish I can visit there some day. By the way, among your flower photos, I found opium flower. Is it allowed to grow opium privately? In my country any kind of narcotic plants are not allowed to be grown privately.

We just have passed through a long and hot summer. Of course, summer is still going on. I mean record-breaking hot weather. From last week there began endurable breeze and temperature dropped a little bit. It was really a terrible heat. My vegetable garden was hard hit by continuing heat and drought.

Thanks to your concern, I am very healthy. My tooth is so-so. But I brush eagerly my tooth three times a day with the toothbrush and paste you sent to me. Thanks again. Now I am practicing a traditional therapy to keep my health. That is urine therapy. You may know this. I drink a cup of my urine, the first one in the morning, everyday. Besides I rinse my mouth with it to strengthen my weak gum. I hope you will not feel disgust to hear this. I know some westerners knew this therapy from long ago. Look up the Old Testament, Proverbs 5, 15–17. It is said that that phrases indicate urine therapy. Anyway, I think I found a very good medicine in the prison, no need [for] money no effort to get. It's very difficult to obtain good medicine properly. Because all inmates must take a medicine which is designated by the prison authority. So you can't send medicine. I'm sorry. And there's no weight restriction in mailing here, but electronics such as radio, watch and razor are not allowed to let in. Because there are so many restrictions when things are brought in from outside. I can't say which one is OK and which one is NO. I hope you understand this. But I tell you one thing to help your understanding; there are very many regulations in an organization, but all the regulations are not abided by exactly. I should have said that my fellow prisoners of [conscience] asked me to thank you for the chocolate and candies you sent to me last Christmas. When we receive something to eat from outside, we make it a rule to share them evenly among colleagues living in the same floor.

I love to see Carl Larsson's paintings. His pen drawing is really marvellous. I think I can learn lot of things from his paintings.

Yes, I can hear bird singing. But they are not my friends. They are too far from me. My best friends are spiders and mantis. They are only living things to watch amusely in my solitary cell. I live and play with them all day long.

Dear Christa, you must be very surprised at the sight of North Korean grief on their leader's death. I'll write about that in the next letter. I wish you are always in good health and God bless you.

From your BAU

January 12, 1997

Dear Mrs. Pauline Neville,

Thank you for your Christmas card. It's been a long time to hear from you. There must have been some mail accidents between you and me. Hoping no more in this year. I'm writing the first letter of 1997 to you.

I am sorry to hear that you broke your arm. Are you alright now? I don't think you wear high-heels in your age. You should wear flat shoes and be careful when running.

Thanks for your concern, I'm very well. Last year was a little tough for me in respects of human relation. I think it was developed from my weak point of personal character. As time goes by being imprisoned, I feel some difficulties in treating people who are very different from me. Is my adaptability deteriorating ... I need refreshment.

These days I indulge in paintings, water-coloring. I was an amateur artist. Last November there was a national prison art exhibition. Two of my paintings were chosen and displayed in a cultural centre near Seoul. I am now preparing to participate in a civilian art exhibition this year.

I hear a record breaking cold wave has struck all over the Europe and over two hundred people died of the cold. I worry about you and your neighbors are safe. In Korea too, this winter is particularly cold. Is it the beginning of another Ice Age? Anyway, I'm still alive and spending the cold days thinking good friends far away. Dear Pauline, I hope you are in good health. Best wishes for 1997!

Yours,

Bau

9 July 1998

Dear Pauline,

I have just received your letter with delight. Thanks for your cheering of Korean soccer team. Although I had cheered England team [eagerly], they lost the game with Argentina regrettably. But they did very well with only ten. I couldn't watch the game.

I could watch TV only one time in a week. So I ask them to tape the highlights (for two hours) of the games of the week. As a result I saw only the scenes of scoring points. The whole game I watched was Korea's third match; against Belgium. Did you see it? They showed real fighting in that game. The manager of Belgium team was dismissed because of this game. If they win by a large score, they might survive the league. The manager Mr. Cha was dismissed halfway on the charge of the first two defeats. Because almost all Koreans eagerly wanted a victory. (Korea participated all five times in World Cup, but never recorded one victory.) Objectively, Mexico and Holland are far stronger than Korea, but national feeling didn't accept such a big defeat. The headless Korean team fought a desperate fight against Belgium and made tie. In doing so, they nearly restore their pride. Obviously Belgium is stronger than Korea, but they became a victim of Korean pride. Brazil and France will fight in the final match. It will be a great match. I predict Brazil will win with many goals.

Oh, Pauline, thank you so much. You sent letter to the Head of Prison for my watching TV. Watching TV freely is impossible in this prison. They provide TV watching for inmates only once a week, and even it is restricted only through VTR.

I have received a book sent by you last week. Thank you much. *Blackfoot Physics*. I am very much interested in indigenous knowledge system. As soon as I glanced over this book, I found

I have really wanted to read. I like those books dealing with the relation between science and spirituality.

I have submitted two water-color paintings for this year's prison art exhibition, which will be held in October. From my judgement the work of this year better than last years. I'm sure they would bear a good result. But I am in happy trouble now. The government announced that there will be a wide range of amnesty on 15 August on the occasion of [the] 50th anniversary of the foundation of ROK [the Republic of Korea]. If I am released next month, I cannot help but take back my paintings. But release is far more important than exhibition. If I am released, I think I can hold my private exhibition.

We are in the middle of monsoon at this moment. We have had long rainy days since June. It's about to end. Then we will have very hot and humid weather during the rest of July and August. Rainy days are not good for inmates because we cannot have exercise hours, which is the only chance of refreshment during the day. But rain gives us another feeling of refreshment.

Dear Pauline, I hope you will have a nice summer holiday and keep fit. I send my warmest greetings to the members of your committee.

God bless you!

Yours,

Bau

18.8.98

Dear Pauline

FREE AT LAST!

FROM Bau, with many thanks.

E-mail from Hwang Dae-Kwon to Lucy Popescu at English PEN 24/2/2002:

Bau is going to get married on the 18 of May at the Suhgang university church in Korea. Although you are not able to come and see, I hope you will congratulate the celebration on that day. I am terribly sorry for not sending any news for a long time. Some might think, Bau has deserted us. Of course not! I have been always thinking of you even in the middle of busy work. I know very well that the current being called Bau is the product of your warm love and prayers. Because of my laziness and ground-less optimism, I have delayed my saying hallo to you. In fact I have been busy since I returned to Korea writing articles and books and giving lectures to various NGOs on the community movement and ecological agriculture. I am still writing for several books that are to be published this year. Here's a good news. On arriving home in October last year I began translating Allan Weisman Gaviotas into Korean. This book is a story about the construction of an eco-village in a remote countryside in Colombia. When the book was on display at the beginning of this month, the book section editors of the major newspapers carried favourable articles for the book. Two major papers, Hankyoreh and Jungang, offered full-page coverage. Thanks to this favourable coverage, my book took the 6th ranking in the political! and social category at the biggest bookshop (Kyobo Book Center) in Korea. This means that Korean people today are eagerly seeking an alternative life in this chaotic develop-ment fever...

Let me tell you about the most curious thing, my fiancée. Her name is Hwang Ae-Kyung Lucia, aged 44. She had been a long time member of a Catholic laywoman community as a professional translator. She broke her pledge (I assure you I never forced her) to make a wife of a man, you know Bau. I have got to know her from the last year of my prison term when she sent me a letter. She is a small woman but has a deep religious faith and warm human nature. Of all things I like her bright character. She always tries to cheer me up and to see things from the positive side. Because of my ailing father, we will stay in my parents' house for the time being. Seeing the development of situation, we have a plan to move to the countryside in the next year or so, where my long cherished dream – building a community farm – will come true. I wish all the best things and send my deepest love to you. I will try to send the Bau Letter from time to time. If you pressure me through your response, it may become a regular correspondence. Yours Bau from Korea. Bau is giving a lecture in the Buddhist Academy for Ecological Awakening. Wedding photo will be next.

Khin Zaw Win

Khin Zaw Win (a.k.a. Kelvin), a dentist, former interpreter, speech- and report-writer for UNICEF, and a student, was arrested on 4 July 1994 and sentenced to fifteen years' imprisonment. He was arrested at Yangon airport, Burma, as he prepared to leave for Singapore and was accused of carrying documents relating to the Burmese opposition movement. Together with other dissidents, Kelvin was accused of having made contact with foreign diplomats and journalists and having sent 'news comments against or critical of the government' to them. He was released in August 2005.

The following is a poem written in prison and dated 5 May 2005.

What I'm doing

What I'm doing
Isn't for ideals or doctrines
Or systems or other gobbledegook
Dished out by the state;
It isn't for the trumpets or the cheers either,
Nor with an eye on
The pages of history:
That exasperating menu
Is for others to slaver after.

I want you to know

That what I'm doing
Is for what's written in your eyes –
The deep wordless intimations
Are the most valid reason
I can find.
For they hold the beginning and the end
Of my long journey,
Every breath and heartbeat of this land,
The anguish and the rapture,
And the hope, for whatever it's worth.

Your eyes beseech the fulfilment
Of the many promises deferred,
The regaining of the chances lost,
Succour for the lives broken.

They narrate in its entirety
The Greek tragedy
That's been treading the boards
This half-century.

Let me reach out and hold you then
For all time,
So that the things I've willed for you
Shall take on substance,
And that which flows from you
Shall transmute
Into the wherewithal.

Ali Reza Jabari

Ali Reza Jabari, an Iranian translator and freelance contributor to several independent newspapers, was arrested on 17 March 2003 and sentenced to four years' imprisonment, 253 lashes and a fine of six million rials for 'consuming and distributing alcoholic drinks' and 'adultery and incitement to immoral acts'. It is thought that he was targeted for his membership of the Iranian Writers' Organization and for making contributions critical of the Iranian authorities to foreign-based news websites. He previously had been arrested on 28 December 2002, his house was searched and his computer hard drive was seized following a critical interview he gave to a Persian language newspaper in Canada. On 17 June 2003 an appeals court upheld the conviction but reduced the prison term from four to three years. Jabari suffers from a heart condition and was said to be denied medical care. Following international pressure Jabari was granted early release on 14 October 2004.

He wrote the following letter to his minder, Trevor Mostyn, from Rajaee-Shahr Prison, Tehran.

Saturday, 15th May, 2004

Dear Trevor Mostyn,

Your letter came to me on Thursday, 12th May 2004, on which day I visited my wife face to face in prison. It had reached her a few days before that. I was very glad to receive your letter a few days after I received letters from Christine O'Brien and Val Warner because I see that you and your fellow-citizen writers are the first of my friends overseas who are in steady correspondence with me since the time I was arrested and put into jail; and that, in contrary with what I had heard of English citizens, I find you and your fellow citizens very kind and warm-hearted friends who are steadfast and persistent in defending human rights, democracy and civil rights and freedoms. I send my wholehearted greetings to you and to the other members of English PEN who welcomed me kindly as an honorary member of their civic society, and to the committee on whose behalf you are writing to me, and I wish to have the best relations with you in the future. You and your fellow citizen Penners are going to make some awareness about what is really going on in prisons in my country; and this encourages me because it reassures me that pure hearts may love each other and may get into contact with each other without geographical boundaries and free of the wills of their states, all over the world.

Thank you for your good wishes for the future of my country, and for your kind and heartfelt ideas about the results of our lives as freedom fighters, and as the defenders of humanism and human rights, and also as truth-seekers; but I believe that the whole life of any human being and the alterations of one's mind and deed in its course proves to what extent one is truly dedicated to one's beliefs, functions and struggle; and I wish to prove by my actions and throughout my life that I am such a person as you wrote about.

The Islamic Republic of Iran and the judicial power in my country keep some political prisoners together in Evin, but political prisoners like me and others are being kept amongst the ordinary prisoners. I think they will be taken to prisons other than Qasr; perhaps to Rajee-Shahr these days. Today, the last party of Qasr prisoners was transferred here, but I may not know whether they have come to this block or not, since the prisoners of each jail can know little or perhaps nothing about one another. In such a jail, we suffer jails in jails; jail sentences by judicial authorities and others by the moralities and behaviours of their fellow prisoners. Besides that they want to pretend that they have no political prisoners; that we are also ordinary criminals, arrested and kept in prison for our forbidden deeds contrasting with Allah's rules; and that we may be united in some kind of conspiracy if we are all kept together.

In each case they behave as their benefit and our loss dictates; sometimes as political and sometimes as ordinary prisoners.

You asked how you can help and support me. I think such support may be offered within the limits of your possibilities, which you know much better than me. But what I may say in this regard, as a victim of authoritarianism and dictatorship, is that we freedom fighters, democracy strugglers and truth-seekers in Iran need some kind of cultural and psychological non-governmental support, paid internationally, by the world intelligentsia. We Iranians are amongst the founders of world culture, and we have a history of civilization more than four thousand years old; but we have been halted at the threshold of modernity for more than 140 years.

What we, as members of the Iranian struggling intelligentsia need, is some kind of campaign by the world intelligentsia which may pull us out of this 'bleak world' or 'situation', as you wrote; and I know that you, the members of the English intelligentsia, will be the forerunners in such a field.

I shall ask my wife to send you some of my translations and articles, including my translation of *The Female Form* by Rosalind Miles, which I myself had to censor, according to conditions in Iran today. Ershad [Ministry of Islamic Culture and Guidance] also censored than fourteen pages and many words and phrases according to orders to change it, to make it agreeable to conservative tastes.

I am glad to know that you have learned the Persian language, and that you adore works by our Iranian classic poets, and modern writers such as Jamalzadeh and Hedayat ... I also admire works by English classic and modernist writers, such as William Shakespeare, Dickens, women writers such as Virginia Woolf and the Brontë sisters. I adore Shakespeare's masterpiece, *Hamlet*, and I have seen the different versions of the films made of it some 7–8 times ...

I thank you for your kind correspondence with me, and look forward to its continuance in the future.

Wholeheartedly yours,

Ali Reza.

Edited by Baqer Moin

Flora Brovina

An Albanian poet, doctor and women's activist from Kosovo, Flora Brovina was arrested in April 1999 in Pristina, where an eyewitness saw her being taken from the house she was staying in by Serb masked paramilitaries, who then drove her away in a car. For some time her whereabouts were unknown and there were fears for her life; news eventually came through that she had been transferred into Serbia, together with around one thousand other Kosovans, and was imprisoned in Pozarevac.

Brovina was given a twelve-year sentence, on charges of alleged links with the Kosovo Liberation Army, although there was no evidence that she had been involved in violence. It was believed that she was held for her public protests against Serb human rights abuses in Kosovo. Brovina had opted to remain in Pristina, throughout the NATO bombing, despite the entry of Serb troops into the city. She visited pregnant women, held a clinic and looked after an orphanage which she established for war orphans.

She received the PEN Barbara Goldsmith Freedom to Write Award in 2000 and was released on 1 November of that year, on the order of the incoming president, Kostunica.

The following poem is translated from FreeB92 Samizdat's collection of Brovina's poems, Nazovi Me Mojim Imenom (Call Me by My Name).

The freedom

The freedom
Bird's-flight
Past the window

Awakening of the dawn
Open-handed

It is
The moon
Behind bars

Freedom
Wheat's fragrance
Just reaped

Children's games
Laughter and tears

It is
The woman
Delivered of the burden

Freedom
Ruddy babe
At the mother's breast

What is it like oh what is it like
The Freedom

Translated by Hans-Joachim Lankstch

Liu Jinsheng

Liu Jinsheng co-edited and distributed *Tansuo* (Explorations) magazine in China in the late 1970s with the well-known dissident Wei Jingsheng, and was involved in peaceful opposition activities. He was arrested on 28 May 1992 and sentenced to fifteen years in prison. He was tried with sixteen others accused of being members of counter-revolutionary organizations, most notably the Chinese Progressive Alliance, Liberal Democratic Party of China and Free Labour Union of China. Liu was specifically accused of having a leading role in the Liberal Party and of drafting and disseminating documents concerning the Preparatory Committee of the Free Labour Union. He was also accused of distributing pro-democracy leaflets around 4 June 1992, and of being involved with the production of the journal *Freedom Forum*. He was released in 2004.

A thanksgiving letter to friends of International PEN from Liu Jingsheng.

Sunday, November 28, 2004, Beijing

Dear PEN friends:

How do you do! I am so glad to have heard, as soon as I got back home, that I have been made an Honorary Member of your PEN centres. This is the first gift that I have received after being in jail for twelve and a half years. This is encouraging to me, as well as an approval of my unremitting fight for freedom and democracy these years.

Because I participated in founding the Liberal Democratic Party of China and appealed to the Chinese Government to be open to freedom of expression and promote democracy in politics, I was arrested on May 27, 1992 and then sentenced to fifteen years' imprisonment. When I was in jail I never gave up my fight for democracy and liberty, nor my efforts to learn knowledge. I persisted in studying political science and law on my own. I took the examinations of law discipline in high self-teaching education and passed twelve special courses. At the same time, I read works of political science written by many famous scholars in the world, and made a lot of notes. I believe prison can only deprive our body from freedom, but it cannot help but give us more space to think freely as well as more time to think about the meaning of life, the personal missions of our lives, and the problems of democracy in Chinese politics. My imprisonment for twelve and a half years has not destroyed my wishes, neither has it stopped my fight for democracy and liberty, nor my longing for knowledge. On the contrary, it tempered my willpower, disciplined my thinking, honed my writing ability, gave me a lot of driving force and material too and, in particular, made me many friends and comrades.

When I was in the jail, some international organizations gave me various awards, which, needless to say, encouraged me spiritually to get over my hard time there. I have been grateful to them for such help and encouragement. When I regained my freedom and learned that I have been made an Honorary Member of your PEN centres, I feel deeply honoured, and it is a great spiritual encouragement to me. I shall never let you and my friends down. I will continue fighting as always and take my steps more and more steadily.

Thanks again!

Your friend sincerely

Jingsheng Liu

Section Two

DEATH

*Imprisoned or persecuted writers may have a premonition
of their own death, as was the case with Ken Saro-Wiwa,
witness the deaths of fellow inmates, or foresee the murder of
dissidents at the hands of government agents. Death comes in
many guises, including starvation, assassination and judicial
execution.*

Ken Saro-Wiwa

Ken Saro-Wiwa was executed by hanging in Nigeria on 10 November 1995. He had been arrested the previous year and charged with incitement to murder. The underlying reason for his arrest and conviction was his outspoken opposition to Nigeria's successive military governments and his defence of the Ogoni people, of which he was a member. The Ogonis live on land that has been environmentally degraded by intensive oil extraction by multinational companies. Ken Saro-Wiwa was one of Nigeria's most beloved writers. His work as a poet, novelist and screenplay writer won both critical and popular acclaim. His novel *Sozaboy* was hailed by the British writer William Boyd as one of the 'finest achievements of African literature'.

What follows are edited extracts from his last work, written in prison on about 5 November 1995, before his execution on 10 November, and smuggled out to PEN. Disturbingly prescient, Saro-Wiwa describes his own death and its aftermath.

On the Death of Ken Saro-Wiwa

Physical torture did not kill me. Nor did mental torture. Then, one night, the ghost arrived. Tall and gangly, dressed in ragged Nigerian Army camouflage uniform, his bones shooting out of holes in his uniform, his brown teeth as huge as tusks projecting from enormous lips, he came to me, automatic weapon slung over his shoulder, a little drum, an Ogoni drum called 'Ekoni', in his hand. He sounded the drum, Ken-ti-mo, Ken-ti-mo, Ken-ti-mo!

The familiar sound of the little drum woke me up. At the sight of the ghost, I laughed. Annoyed by my laughter, he dropped the drum and laid hold of his automatic weapon. He pointed it at me at close range. I did not flinch. He cocked the weapon and fingered the trigger. I did not bat an eyelid.

'Who are you?' I asked.

'I'm General Jeno Saidu.'

'Sounds like genocide to me,' I said.

'You should know.'

'What do you want?' I asked.

'I'm here to finish you,' replied he, in a gruff voice.

'General, stop swaggering. You do not impress me.'

'You will be impressed. I've finished all your Ogoni people – men, women and children. Once I deal with you, my task is done.'

'Go ahead,' I challenged him.

'You are not afraid to die?'

'No.'

'Why not?'

'I'm prepared to go with all my people whom you confess to having already murdered.'

'Yes, I worked hard on them. I made short work of them. All five hundred thousand of them. You are the last man.'

'So go ahead.'

General Jeno Saidu, the ghost, shot into the ceiling. I laughed.

'Why did you shoot into the ceiling and not into my chest?'

'You're still not afraid?'

'No, General.'

'And why not?'

'Because I have what is greater than your weapon.'
Whereupon, I said, after the English poet Blake:

'I will not cease my mental fight

Nor shall my pen sleep in my hand

Till we have built a new Ogoni

In Niger delta's wealthy land.'

Then I drew my pen from under my pillow. The General's
weapon fell from his hand, and he slumped to his knees ...

When the news came that Ken Saro-Wiwa had given up the
ghost in the offices of the State Investigation and Intelligence
Bureau in Port Harcourt, there was a flurry in newspaper houses
in Lagos as in many other places in Nigeria and abroad. I was
hurriedly dispatched to cover the story.

I found, on arrival in Port Harcourt, that the funny little man
had given up the ghost a few days after this interrogation by
men of the Federal Investigation and Intelligence Bureau from
Lagos, leaving behind an epitaph to be put on his gravestone,
and a hurriedly written note explaining why he had decided to
give up the ghost.

His presence in the office of the State Investigation and
Intelligence Bureau is explained by the fact that he was refused
accommodation in the dingy, damp, smelly guardroom where
men in police custody were normally kept. Senior police officers
who knew their onions and had information of the plot against
the man decided that they would not have his blood on their
hands. Eventually they found him a place in an office where he
bathed, ate and slept – for three nights running – and was able
to write his story as advised by the ghost.

There was great jubilation at Government House, Port
Harcourt, the headquarters of the notorious Rivers State Internal
Security Task Force. Champagne bottles popped endlessly.
Military buffoons gleamed. Boots shone. The Commander of

the Task Force shook hands with the Military Administrator. The former knew that he would soon be promoted to the rank of General. The latter knew that his position was secure and he would soon be nominated to Nigeria's highest-ranking body, the Provisional Ruling Council. The Task Force had successfully completed the genocide of the Ogoni people.

All that was left was to dispose of Mr Saro-Wiwa's corpse. There was a debate as to how best to carry out this task. In the first place, there were none of his relatives alive, all Ogoni people, men, women and children having fallen to the gallant troops led by the deadly ghost, General Jeno Saidu. The telephone to his house and office had been cut to deprive his family of sustenance and ruin his business. His poor family had fled to London before they could be murdered. This knotty problem was solved when it was decided that it was a Task and therefore the Internal Security Task Force should be assigned the responsibility.

Next was where he should be buried. This question was quickly settled. The entire Ogoni territory had become a cemetery. The hundred thousand Ogoni people had all been buried. Ken Saro-Wiwa would cap the mass burial ceremony.

So, as is usual in Nigeria, a contract was awarded for the burial of the little man. The officer who won the contract for supplying the coffin, to maximize his profit for the deal, decided to hire a carpenter to make it. He gave the coffin-maker precise instructions. The coffin had to be no more than five feet long and one foot wide. The shocked carpenter succeeded in making the coffin to specification. But, being a Nigerian, and therefore innumerate, he actually made it two inches shorter either way. This also saved money.

Poor Ken was squashed into this contraption. And being used to protesting against injustice, his corpse squeaked and screamed. The officer who had won the contract for putting Ken in the coffin ran for his dear life. So the Military Administrator had to do the job himself. He duly cancelled this aspect of the contract and demoted the officer for cowardice.

Then the soldiers who were to act as pall-bearers refused to do the job alleging that they had not been paid their Ration Cash Allowance (RCA) for exterminating the Ogoni people. The Commander of the Task Force paid the money on the spot, and the bier was borne through Port Harcourt to show all the residents and other Nigerians what it costs to demand an end to environmental degradation and pollution by oil companies, and social justice for the poor and oppressed.

When the funeral procession got to Ogoni territory, it was no surprise to find Shell, Saipem, Ferrostaal, Chevron, and a gaggle of industrial oil contractors from Europe and America. This helped to give the burial of the little man a well-deserved international flavour since he had made it a point to complain to the international community about the dehumanization and denigration of the Ogoni people and other peoples of the Niger delta.

Shell and Chevron, who have oil-mining leases covering the whole of Ogoni territory, chose the exact spot where the funny little man was to be buried. Care had to be taken, they said, because all the Ogoni land was a huge oil well and now that human beings, flora, fauna and all had been disposed of, oil exploitation could go on without let or hindrance or protests about ecological war, double standards, hypocrisy, acid rain, gas flaring and all.

The right size of hole was dug – tiny and narrow, no more than five foot by one. And the coffin was lowered, and wait for it, stood upright – to save space. Which fulfilled Ken's prophecy in his epitaph which was duly laid on the grave:

Here stands the funny little sweet
The Nigerians loved to cheat
So much so that e'en in death
They denied him six feet of earth.

As the procession made to go, a message flashed across the sky like lightning: 'Congratulations, congratulations to the Internal Security Task Force. Your success has won for Nigeria unanimous election to Permanent Membership of the United Nations Security Council.'

And Ken Saro-Wiwa laughed in his grave.

Thiagarajah Selvanithy

Thiagarajah Selvanithy (Selvi) was a drama student at the University of Jaffna as well as a poet, campaigner for women's rights and the editor of a feminist magazine in Sri Lanka. She was abducted from her home on 30 August 1991 by members of the Liberation Tigers of Tamil Eelam (LTTE or Tamil Tigers), and in October 1993 a spokesman admitted that she was being held by the guerrilla forces. Selvi's abduction appeared to be linked to her criticism of the guerrilla movement. In 1997 LTTE sources acknowledged that she had been executed.

The following is a poem received by PEN.

Undying gardens[1]

I've grown feeble.
Do not bother me with questions.
My heart that hangs on a thread
will fall and explode
any moment.

The asoka garden isn't something dead
in the past.

---

1 In the epic *Ramayana*, Ravana·is the demon of Lanka who abducts Sita and imprisons her in a garden of asoka trees. Rama, the hero and her husband, lays siege to Lanka and manages to rescue Sita. Selvi's poem plays with the idea of the husband turning into the captor.

This very house
is an asoka garden made specially for me.
But my captor
is not Ravana, but Rama himself.

That moment when I happened to see
Rama change into Ravana
turning his back on me,
changing his mask,

My heart shuddered.
Who will come now to rescue this Sita?

How long will these asoka trees last?

Translated by A. K. Ramanujan

Rakhim Esenov

Rakhim Esenov is a writer and journalist in Turkmenistan. He was arrested by members of the Ministry of National Security (MNB) on 23 February 2004 for interrogation. During questioning, Esenov suffered a stroke and was taken to hospital, where he remained under security service guard. Two days later he was transferred to the MNB investigation–interrogation unit. He was released on condition that he would not leave the country, and was warned against continuing to report for Radio Free Europe/Radio Liberty.

On 2 March 2004 Esenov was accused of 'inciting social, national and religious hatred', on charges related to his book *Ventsenosny Skitalets* (*The Crowned Wanderer*), banned in Turkmenistan for ten years. The book was published in Moscow in 2003 and 800 copies were delivered to Esenov's home. In January 2004, customs authorities removed the books, claiming they had been imported illegally.

The book is set in the Mogul Empire, founded in the sixteenth century, and centres on Bayram Khan, a poet, philosopher and army general, said to have saved Turkmenistan from fragmentation. In 1997 the late President Saparmurat Niyazov denounced the book as being 'historically inaccurate' and demanded that corrections be made, which Esenov refused to do.

The following is an edited extract from Ventsenosny Skitalets (The Crowned Wanderer).

The death of the poet

Bayram Khan, with a scarf tied around his neck as a sign of obedience and repentance, fell to his knees at the sovereign's feet. Akbar lifted Bayram Khan's face; he wanted to say something, but the lump in his throat prevented him. The emperor embraced him, seizing him by the shoulders, untied the scarf from the poet's neck, dried the tears off the poet's face, and sat him on his right, as his deputy. To the left of the emperor sat Munim-Khan, Bayram Khan's successor.

The sovereign conversed with the Khan of Khans deep into the night; he was all attention and courtesy. Akbar gave his former tutor the robe of honour which he took off his own shoulder, and then laid out to him the various options: if the career of military general tempted him, then he could go into the *dzhagir*[1] of Kalpa and Chandera, where he would pursue the conquest of Khindustan. If he chose to serve at court, then he could become a *musakhib*, a trusted advisor of the sovereign. And finally, the third choice was a pilgrimage. 'You were in the services of the Chagatai dynasty for forty years,' Akbar said solemnly. 'You faithfully served three of its Tsars, you are the hero of Machkhivara and Sirkhind; your military leadership brought victory and glory to the Mogul army under Panipat. For a long time you expertly manoeuvred the national ship along the waves of life ... If you prefer to stay in Khindustan, as a *musakhib* under the emperor, we will regard this decision favourably and make you the benefactor of our family. And if you are more inclined to seek consolation in solitude, we will help you complete a pilgrimage to Mecca, giving you escorts of your choice.'

Bayram Khan listened attentively to the sovereign's speech.

---

1 The prevailing form of feudal land ownership during the Mogul era of India.

He noticed that the sovereign did not even once call him 'khan-baba', as he had before; he was hiding his eyes, refusing to meet the poet's intense gaze. Akbar's indifferent manner of speech seemed forced, as if fulfilling an obligation. It was as if this whole meeting was for show; the sovereign's words did not contain any of their previous honesty and warmth, he had become totally alien ... He seemed to be offering the service with the *dzbagirs* and the post of *musakhib* with a certain reluctance, or, as the Turkmen say, just 'paying lip service'. But when proposing the pilgrimage to Mecca he was insistent, and it was obvious he really wanted to send the poet all the way there. The emperor rushed to say that he would be given 53,000 rupees in cash to spend, and be escorted through Khindustan by the Khadzha Mukhammed Khan Seistan and Dursun-Bey – emirs Bayram Khan had always trusted.

Bayram Khan, having thanked the emperor, announced that he was choosing the path of the Hadji,[2] and felt more at ease. He was surprised at himself: he did not want to stay one more day at court, in this cesspool. He would have had to wear the tight *bovsug* again, the iron collar of courtier, play the hypocrite and lead a double life ... how vexing that decades of one's life pass before one realizes that a poet who becomes a courtier of the highest order has to lead a double existence. That is why court poets who occupied state functions wrote very little, if they wrote at all; and if they did it was for one man only – their leader, at whose hand the court poet was fed and watered.

The clever ruler, knowing the dual nature of the Poet, is always trying to draw him nearer to himself. There is a wise saying: 'A ruler who does not befriend a Poet is a fool, but a Poet who tries to befriend a ruler is twice as stupid.' This is obviously why many poets, who know their own worth, preferred the wild

---

2 Muslim who has been to Mecca.

canyons of the deserted mountains, the depths of deserts and the dusty paths of dervishes to the brilliance and luxury of palaces.

Only now did Bayram Khan comprehend the wisdom of this philosophy. Knowing that he was considered dangerous and objectionable at court, he did not hesitate in making his choice: he would go and worship in holy Mecca, and he would distribute the 50,000 rupees he had received from the government to the poor and needy he would meet on his way to Arabia.

Finally they decided to take to the road. Bayram Khan, bidding farewell to the places he loved, took a boat on the lake, to go hunting one more time. He spent almost the whole day in the wild. On his way back to camp, Bayram Khan noticed on the shores of the lake a familiar servant of the town ruler, who made him a sign. Thinking that he had been sent by this ruler, Bayram Khan ordered the boatman to moor the boat.

The weather started to spoil as he approached the shore. It was not yet the time of *saratan*, the month during which strong winds blow and heavy rains pour on Khindustan. The sky became overcast, the wind picked up, creating sharp ripples on the calm surface of the lake, bending the coastal reeds where the ducks and all that was alive around the lake were rushing to hide. The sky opened and the first large drops of rain fell onto the earth.

Bayram Khan, protecting the edges of his robe from the gusts of wind, stepped onto the shore. Horsemen, from their appearance probably Afghans, emerged from the coastal grove. They hurriedly bypassed the Khan of Khans. A young Afghan in a rich *chapan* [heavily quilted robe], his face sullen, led the way. He came over to Bayram Khan, with his right hand behind his back.

Bayram Khan, not in the least suspicious, and thinking

that the Afghans had come to offer him a gift of honour, light-heartedly extended his hand to greet them. They all greeted him apart from the leader. The latter, still holding his right hand behind his back, was not offering his left hand, and only then was doubt born in the heart of Bayram Khan: 'Is this … my death? … Oh Allah, how easy it all is …'

'Do you know me?' the young Afghan asked sharply, fixing the Khan of Khans with his cold gaze.

'No, I have not had the honour …'

'Well I know you, Bayram Khan …'

'We had better start by introducing ourselves. Indeed, every Muslim comes from Allah.'

'How can one greet a murderer? I am Mubarek Khan, son of the Malik Lokhan, whom you condemned to death under Panipat. Did you know that?!'

'I did. But he died in battle, around Khemu …'

Bayram Khan knew Lokhan very well; the latter had been a fierce enemy of the moguls. At the beginning he had served Babur, then the Sher-shakha, but when he died, Lokhan had crossed over to the Mirza Kamrana. Lokhan had industriously served the Mirza – even though he was a hateful Timurid, he was born of an Afghan mother. After the defeat of Kamran, Lokhan had run to Dehli, and served under the banner of the ill-starred guardians of Sher-shah, until the triumphant Khemu appeared on the horizon.

Bayram Khan remembered Lokhan clearly: he had seen him more than once in the company of the Karman. He had also seen him dead in the Panipat field. Someone had mistaken him for the dead Khemu, and transported Lokhan's corpse to the tent of the military general.

'No! You killed him!' Mubarek Khan blazed up.

'Here, read,' the voice of an old Afghan came from behind; he handed over a filthy piece of paper. 'Here it is: in your handwriting, the *firman*[3] giving the order to execute the Malik Lokhan. They brought it to us from Dehli. Our trusted people sent it over ...'

Bayram Khan turned towards where the voice was coming from, and was extending his arm towards the piece of paper, when Mubarek Khan, letting out a wild roar, expertly struck him in the back with a quick move of the dagger. The strike was so strong that the edge of the blade came out of his chest. Bayram Khan, gulping for air, stared at his attacker in disbelief; he still stood firmly on his feet, until the elderly Afghan, trying to hack his head off, struck him in the back of the head with his sword. Tumbling head first onto the ground, Bayram Khan pronounced but two words: 'Allah Akbar ...' After the last gasps of his death-rattle, the dead poet, flooded in his own blood, lay for a long time in the roadside dust.

Thunder rumbled, lightning flashed, illuminating with pale blue flames the dark clouds hanging low, which burst into heavy showers. The rain poured down onto Bayram Khan's lifeless body for a long time, as if it realized that there was no one to bathe the *shekhit* [martyr] – the just and pious man who perished on his way to the holy Kaaba.

Translated by Rachel Segonds

---

3 Royal mandate or decree

Angel Cuadra

The poet Angel Cuadra served a fifteen-year prison sentence in Cuba (see also p. 64).

The following poem was written in prison in Cuba.

A man dies, Cuba, 1964

A man dies obscurely ...
he is gasping and dying,
gulping sad cups of smoke.
Muddy rain falls slowly onto his soul.
He starts to shout – and vomits out a curse of hate;
to look – and his eyes are scratched by filth;
to fly – and hits the limits of his allotted space.

A man is hugging death
beneath his armpit,
gnawing a macabre bone.
Through clogged lungs, he breathes spider-webs.
He is thirsty, and light seems a distant well.

A man dies obscurely;
breathes, stands upright though wounded:
Cuba casts a troubled glance into the hollow of his cell.

Translated by Ruth Fainlight

Akbar Ganji

Iranian Akbar Ganji is the author of *Dungeon of Ghosts*, a collection of articles published in early 2000, in which he implicated leading conservative figures in the 'serial murders' of several dissidents and intellectuals in 1998. The book is thought to have been a major factor in the conservative defeat in the parliamentary elections of February 2000.

The writer was arrested following his participation in an academic and cultural conference held in Berlin in April 2000, at which political and social reform in Iran were publicly debated. In January 2001 Ganji was sentenced to ten years' imprisonment plus five years' internal exile, for various charges, including attendance at the conference. Although an appeal court reduced his sentence to six months, the Tehran judiciary brought new charges against him in connection with articles written prior to April 2000. Ganji was sentenced in July 2001 to six years' imprisonment for 'collecting confidential information harmful to national security' and 'spreading propaganda against the Islamic system'. He was granted a conditional release for the Iranian New Year in March 2006.

The following are two extracts from Dungeon of Ghosts. *Ganji's articles were originally published in Iranian newspapers between January and September 1999 – the newspapers were subsequently banned in 2000. According to official statements the main suspect in the 1998 serial killings was Sa'id Emami, who, together with his accomplices, was detained. However, in June 1999 – before any trial had taken place – Emami reportedly committed suicide in prison. The suicide was considered suspicious by Ganji, amongst others, who called for a thorough investigation and for the facts to be made public. The terms 'master key' (to the 'dungeon of ghosts', i.e. the mastermind behind the killings), 'éminence grise' etc. are used by Ganji to refer to the unnamed powerful state officials who – he believes – ordered and organised the serial killings.*

Assassinations' Directors

Originally published in the *Sobh-e Emrouz* newspaper on 7 January 1999

The exposure, by the president's investigation committee, of the operational group that was behind the killing of writers and dissidents is laudable. And we must salute the Intelligence Ministry's courage and sense of responsibility in announcing openly that a number of its personnel were involved in the recent killings. This kind of sense of responsibility cannot be seen in any [other] Third World country and is a result of Iran's civil movement and the integrity of Khatami, who, from the start, insisted on citizens' rights, freedom of expression, the right to express opposing views in the framework of the law, political development, etc.

'Retributive law', which emphasizes the punishment of the offender, rules that the killers be punished as soon as possible. But the aim of modern 'corrective law' is to restore the course of things to justice and fairness. In a modern society, anomalies and offences must be corrected in such a way as to establish order and to reduce the likelihood of the repetition of offences.

The fundamental and important question is this: how must

the problem of the recent crimes be dealt with so that tragedies of this kind absolutely cannot recur?

First, it has been claimed: 'A judicial unit, with three righteous judges – after holding trials *in absentia* – ruled that the liquidated individuals were Corruptors of the Earth and sentenced them to death.'[1] If this claim is correct, the said judges must be detained as soon as possible and, after being made public, they must be punished.

Second, killers receive orders from commanders. The one who pulls the trigger, strangles someone or slashes a body with a knife is an executor. 'The assassination committee' issues the command to kill. It is not enough to identify the killers. The directors must be identified and punished.

The directors do not necessarily reside in the Intelligence Ministry. Ill-minded political losers can, from the outside, influence elements and make them carry out assassinations. The directors are eager that the killers are dealt with rapidly so that their role is expunged from people's minds. Directing everyone's eyes towards the Intelligence Ministry is an optical illusion. The ill-minded bloodsuckers in the field of thought and politics must be identified regardless of their guise or position.

Third, for several years now, the 'discourse of violence' has been intensely propagated from pulpits and newspapers in this land. The discourse of violence provides ideological justifications for the physical elimination of dissident thinkers and activists. It is the duty of the wise, and the mission of the thoughtful, to challenge the 'ideology of violence' and, by deconstructing it, reveal its overt and covert dimensions.

---

1 This quote is taken from a statement issued by a group known as Devotees of Mostafa Navvab's Pure Muhammadan Islam, which was published in *Sobh-e Emrouz* on 5 January 1999; Mostafa Navvab was responsible for a number of political assassinations during the Shah's time. 'Corruptors of the Earth' and 'Warriors against God' are Arabic terms from Islamic jurisprudence; they are offences that are punishable by death.

Lawmakers have a duty to consider the propagation of violence and physical punishment as an offence, so that no one can support violence, especially in the name of defending religion.

Fourth, we must seek assistance from sociology and psychology. Social conditions cause the emergence and spread of violence. Using the theory of the 'authoritarian personality' and the notion of 'failure-aggression', psychology demonstrates the sort of individuals absorbed into violent movements.

Unfortunately, in our society, the social conditions for the growth of fascist movements do exist, and there are also individuals whose psychological disposition drives them into fascist movements.

Fifth, in order to defend religiosity, our *ulema* and religious leaders must combat the proponents of violence; they must not allow them to set up the market stall of murder and crime in the realm of religiousness or to raise the flag of terror on religion's dome.

Throughout Shi'i history, religious leaders have been a refuge for the wronged, and our religious leaders are beyond reproach in this respect. But the great fear is that their silence will be taken as consent and that it will strengthen criminals' resolve and drive young people away from religion.

The Questions Raised by a Suicide[2]

Originally published in the *Sobh-e Emrouz* newspaper on 21 June 1999

1. Last autumn's serial killings and the Shock of 1999 (the

---

2 Translator's note: Gholamhoseyn Mohseni-Ezhe'i was the head of the Special Court for Clergy and the head of the Court for Government Employees – which also deals with press trials – at the time when Akbar

statement issued by the Intelligence Ministry, declaring that some of the ministry's personnel had carried out the killings) sparked the hope that Khatami was standing bravely and firmly in defence of people's rights and that he would extract the blood-sucking leeches from their hidden corners and reveal their ugly faces to citizens; that he would remove the cancerous tumour from the patient's body like a skilled surgeon and, by bringing about structural changes, place state bodies at the service of national interests and the interests of the public.

Before much time had passed from the press's efforts to follow up this tragic incident, a 'decree' arrived: to ensure that the killings are investigated in a calm atmosphere and all the perpetrators and the people involved are identified, made known to the public and openly put on trial; [the press must] remain silent and do not spread 'rumours'; and if you have any 'information', pass it on to the investigation committee only and absolutely no one else.

The press, for their part, lowered their torch from the killings' dungeon of ghosts, simply for the sake of the national interest and in order to assist 'the legitimate government'.

2. One of the dangers that could be sensed when the affair was exposed – and highlighted openly by the press – was that the 'key agent' would commit suicide in prison.

3. I was a prisoner in Evin prison for three months in the winter of 1998. There is nothing available in solitary confinement with

Ganji wrote this article. Mohseni-Ezhe'i is now intelligence minister in President Mahmoud Ahmadinejad's government. Ruhollah Hosseinian, a cleric, was a good friend of Sa'id Emami (the man arrested in connection with the serial killings, who reportedly committed suicide in prison). Hosseinian made a series of very controversial remarks in relation to the serial killings, most notably in two interviews – one with the *Kayhan* newspaper and the other with Iranian state TV – on 11 January 1999.

which to commit suicide. Once every half hour, the guard looks into the cell through the peephole and surveys the prisoner with his 'all-embracing eyes'. When I was in prison, bathing was allowed only once a week, lasting five minutes, under strict supervision, with the guard having the prisoner in full view the whole time.

This is how they treated prisoners who were in jail on press- or politics-related charges, drugs charges, embezzlement, etc. It goes without saying that the 'golden key' [Sa'id Emami] to the dungeon required special supervision and this is something of which the Intelligence Ministry's experts were fully aware. Hence, if there was some oversight and if Sa'id Emami really did commit suicide by swallowing some cleaning substance, all those who allowed this to happen through their negligence are guilty in this affair and must answer for their actions to the noble Iranian people. In order to remove all suspicion, an investigation committee must immediately investigate how Sa'id Emami committed suicide and make their findings public. The people have a right to know.

4. Sa'id Emami's suicide will raise many questions and, if judiciary officials do not clearly answer all the questions, rumours will spread and trust in the ruling system will be seriously tarnished.

Some of the questions that must be officially answered are as follows:

One, what was Sa'id Emami's professional background?

Two, when did Sa'id Emami first enter the Intelligence Ministry?

Three, under which intelligence minister was Sa'id Emami promoted and given the post of deputy minister?

Four, is the Intelligence Ministry's structure such that someone like Sa'id Emami can plan and carry out killings like these using special prerogatives without coming under suspicion?

Five, who were the like-minded people with whom Sa'id Emami associated and by whom he was influenced?

Six, when is the open trial of the [remaining] suspects due to begin?

Seven, how much longer must the press remain silent and not publish people's questions?

In the next stage, the individuals who have not been arrested yet must be certain that the hand of fate will seek them out and that God will wreak vengeance on them, in totally unexpected ways, on behalf of their innocent victims.

But the lesson that Iran's civil movement must learn is that many of our society's key problems are rooted in killings such as these. We must direct our minds towards the serial killings and seek the 'master key' [the mastermind]. If the master key is uncovered and tried openly, many of the secrets of the 'dungeon of ghosts' will be revealed. The aim is not vengeance; the aim is to create conditions in which no one will allow themselves to achieve their aims by spreading violence and terror.

Translated by Nilou Mobasser

Flora Brovina

An Albanian poet, doctor and women's activist from Kosovo, Flora Brovina was arrested in April 1999 in Pristina, where an eyewitness saw her being taken from the house she was staying in by Serb masked paramilitaries who then drove her away in a car. She was eventually released on 1 November 2000 (see p. 129).

The following poem is translated from FreeB92 Samizdat's collection of Brovina's poems, Nazovi Me Mojim Imenom (Call Me by My Name)*.*

The first lesson

Jusuf
Jusuf Amber Stork
Jusuf Gërvalla ... missing
Teuta Ilir Agron Yll
Fadil Fadil Talla ... missing
Ylfete Ylfete Humolli ... missing
Shukrije Shukrije Obërqinca ... missing
Kimete Arsim Kujtim
Halim Halim ... missing
Shpresa Besa Kastriot
Fatmir Fatmir Kërleshi ... missing
Afrim Afrim Zhitia ... missing
Let's go on
Valbone Shkurte Gjon

Xhevat Xhevat ... missing
There's missing Nesimi Bekim
Afrim Afrim Prebreza ... missing

Don't bring along
Certificates
Neither medical
Nor parental or governmental ones
Nor by the police
Just say 'missing'
We'll treat their wounds with flowers
We'll wait for them
We'll wait for them
Just say 'missing'
Blood-red poppy will blossom
The lesson goes on ...

9.5.1990

Translated by Hans-Joachim Lankstch.

Harry Wu

Harry Wu was born in Shanghai, China, in 1937. He was arrested as a student for speaking out against the Soviet invasion of Hungary and criticizing the Chinese Communist Party. In 1960, he was sent to the Laogai – the Chinese Gulag – as a 'counter-revolutionary rightist'. During the next nineteen years, he was imprisoned in twelve different forced-labour camps around China. He survived beatings, torture and starvation, and witnessed the death of many of his fellow prisoners from brutality, disease, starvation and suicide.

Wu arrived in the United States in 1985. He began writing about his experiences in the Laogai, which is the most extensive forced-labour and thought-reform camp system in the world.

During the 1990s, Harry Wu made several trips to China to document the human rights abuses of the Laogai. In 1995, the Chinese government arrested him, and after sixty-six days of captivity he was convicted of 'stealing state secrets', sentenced to fifteen years, and then expelled as the result of an international campaign launched on his behalf.

The following is an extract from his autobiography, Thunderstorm in the Night *(2004), about his experience of labour camps in China in the 1960s–70s.*

In November, Chen Ming died.

My brain cells were gradually deactivating. All varieties of thoughts and perceptions – memories of childhood, nostalgic recollections of my sweetheart, thoughts of missing my parents, the yearning for freedom, the pursuit of dignity, fear of death, bewilderment over hunger – were receding. My brain was empty; it contained nothing, wanted nothing, feared nothing. It was truly blank.

Especially with respect to hunger, I no longer suffered as much. It seemed as if I had no appetite to speak of. The little bit of food I received every day seemed completely normal. What was the fragrance of oil, the taste of meat, sweet and sour? I seemed to have lost my sense of taste. More important, I did not feel hungry. My stomach and intestines had adapted to these conditions. The number of people who died after collapsing in the outhouse during bouts of diarrhoea dwindled. Now, more people died on the *kangs* [sleeping platforms] in their cell blocks, departing without a word.

In the several days before Chen Ming's death, he once again became talkative. I said to him, 'What's the matter with you? You may have the strength to speak, but I don't have the strength to listen to you!'

But he continued to speak, on and off, one sentence short and the next sentence long.

'When I came to Beijing ... I wanted to be a teacher. My girlfriend and I grew up together in the same village. Peasants were looked down on ... in the village middle school, I was a good student ... I loved her. I made a wish that I could become a teacher, then return home to marry her. My uncle lived in Beijing ... Later, I taught geography in a middle school ... on the map, I told my students, Fujian is my home; my fiancée is there ... Taiwan is across from Fujian. Taiwan is a beautiful island ... the people of Taiwan are very brave ... without support from outside, they resisted the Dutch and Japanese invaders ... they are the pride of China ... Later, my girlfriend married somebody else ... then, my mother came to Beijing. I took her to Tiananmen Square for amusement ... we were separated by someone ... I was captured and forced onto a jeep by plain-clothes men ... entered the Public Security Bureau ... then ... Public Security said I spread counter-revolutionary propaganda to the students and opposed the liberation of Taiwan ...'

In my stupor, I half listened. My eyes covered with a towel, I did not even turn my head. I don't know how long he went on.

At the second meal the next day, around 4 p.m., Scar Wang came banging the iron barrels – Clang clang! Clang clang! – to bring us our food. Chen Ming did not sit up; had he been someone I didn't know, as with the one on the other side of my bedroll several days earlier, I would simply have said, 'Scar Wang! Another one over here.' I would not have gone over to nudge him, and I would not have been the slightest bit agitated.

But this was Chen Ming, my only companion in this part of my life. How could he go? How? But I'd been absolutely confident that he would die, just as I believed I would. There was not the slightest notion of chance or doubt. However, in that moment, I could not believe it. I shook him. I believed he must be in a lethargic sleep, that he was too lazy to get up. No! Get up quick! You can't miss your meal! If you don't get up, the others won't allow me to save this portion for you! Get up! Get up! Chen Ming! I want to hear you keep on talking. Come on, get up!

He had really gone to sleep and not got up again.

'Hey, Scar Wang!' I said.

'Hmm ...?'

'Another one over here.'

'He's a friend of yours?' asked Wang.

Not wanting to speak any further, I lay down. The world was so quiet.

In November in the north, the sky is already very dark by

five o'clock in the afternoon. Two duty prisoners came in. One got up on the kang, and one stood at the edge of the kang. Chen Ming was already lying straight with his head under the covers. The two men grabbed the sheets, twisted them at the ends, and carried him out.

In Chen Ming's space on the kang, all that remained were two thin books of some sort or another and an old envelope. I shoved these things under my pillow, and returned to my reclining position. I had no tears, felt no pain.

I don't know how many hours later it was that I heard a duty prisoner outside the cell block crying out in terror. By then, no matter what had happened, it would never have alarmed anyone in the cell block. Everyone continued to lie there quietly.

Our cell block had a window that looked out on a small low house which may have originally been a tool shed. Beginning in September, that house had become a mortuary. Everyone who died in the various groups and detachments was sent to that little house first; then, every morning, an ox cart would come to take all of the corpses away at once. In September, I had seen an ox cart stop in front of the door to that little house; an old duty prisoner unlocked the door, and the duty prisoners that had come on the ox cart entered the house and brought out several flimsy caskets and loaded them on the cart, then the cart left. In October, I had seen the ox cart take away seven or eight corpses wrapped in their bedding. In November, I no longer had the strength to sit up, so I hadn't seen the ox cart. When Chen Ming left me, he, too, had gone to that little house.

After the duty prisoner's screams, I heard the captain arrive. There was more yelling, and before long, they carried someone into our cell block, and placed him in the empty space next to me.

It was Chen Ming!

'What's going on?' I half rose from the bed and asked the duty prisoner.

'Old Zhuang of the mortuary cried out because he saw the door of that little house move and a hand extend out of it. All there was in the morgue were six or seven corpses; how could there be someone alive in there? Old Zhuang said that he'd seen a ghost; he was scared to death, so he started screaming. There used to be one ox cart each day in the morning that took the corpses away, but now it has changed to one in the morning and one in the afternoon. But these corpses arrived after dinner, so they had to wait until morning. Luckily, it's cold, so there isn't any odour. Old Zhuang immediately called the captain, who opened the door and saw Chen Ming lying on the floor in front of the door. Apparently, he hasn't …'

Yama, the King of Hell, is truly conscientious and meticulous; he must have ordered the official in charge of the life and death register to check the rolls, and, discovering that Chen Ming's time had not yet come, sent him back to the world of the living. Just as I had these thoughts, the captain came in, laughing, and said, 'Yama had the wrong name, Chen Ming's time hasn't come. Is everything in order?'

'Uh, Captain, sir.' I sat up and said, 'Chen Ming missed dinner. It should be made up to him.' This was the only thing I could do to help my friend.

The captain asked, 'How do you know he didn't eat?'

'Captain, sir, you can ask the kitchen's Scar Wang,' I said. 'He can verify that Chen Ming "died" before the meal began.'

'The meal is over. If he missed it, he missed it. He'll have to wait until tomorrow,' the captain said with grim determination.

'Captain, what has just happened to Chen Ming is remarkable. As you just said, he has returned from King Yama's grasp. How often does that happen? If you don't give him this meal, he might really have to report to King Yama,' I replied, equally determined.

The captain hesitated a moment, then said, 'All right!' He turned to the duty prisoner and said, 'Get Scar Wang in here!'

It wasn't long before Scar Wang appeared. 'Eh? Chen Ming's back?'

'What,' said the captain, 'do you think we should do?'

'How about this?' the captain said to me. 'You write a note, and I will see what I can do.'

These captains generally had very little education; a good many of them were unable to write official documents or letters. I wrote, 'This is to declare that Chen Ming of Group Six, Detachment Ten, missed the evening meal today with cause. We will be most grateful if you would please understand and exercise forbearance in this matter by reissuing a meal to him.'

The captain took the note, and told Scar Wang, 'Come with me!'

I lay down again, and looked at Chen Ming. His narrow little eyes were closed, and there appeared to be a little moisture on the sparse fuzz on his upper lip; he breathed weakly. Ah! He was still alive, miserable, but alive!

About an hour later, Scar Wang came back. As soon as he entered the room, I sensed an unusual scent; our noses were extremely sensitive to this kind of smell.

'Here, this is for you!'

Scar Wang held a plate on which were placed two steaming *wotous*. One look at them and you could tell that they were real cornmeal wotous, the kind of cornmeal wotous that we called 'golden pagodas'.

Surprised, I said, 'What happened? Scar Wang?'

'This is really unusual,' said Scar Wang. 'The captain took me to the Branch Office. First, he took an official seal out of his jacket pocket and affixed it to the note you wrote. Then he went to the branch director. They spoke for a while, then the branch director approved the note. The captain took me to the cadre's kitchen, and measured out four ounces of cornmeal. I steamed them myself.'

'Chen Ming! Chen Ming! Get up!' I really wanted to help him up with my arms, but I didn't have the strength. 'Hurry! Get up! Look! Look at this!'

Chen Ming didn't move; he just opened his eyes slightly. Scar Wang held the plate out in front of Chen Ming's face and waved it back and forth. 'Look! These are for you! They're yours!'

Suddenly, Chen Ming sat up straight. His eyes widened, and he stared at those two 'golden pagodas'.

'Mine?'

Without waiting for further confirmation, he grabbed the wotous and began shoving them into his mouth; he quickly picked the crumbs from his face, his hands and even his bedding and devoured them as well. In all, it took less than a minute.

Satisfied, he lay down. Scar Wang stared open-mouthed as Chen Ming ate the wotous; when he was finished, Scar Wang left.

Not more than ten minutes after he'd finished the special batch of 'golden pagodas', Chen Ming grabbed his stomach and cried, 'It hurts! … It hurts!' Before he could say it a third time, his body relaxed and he lay flat. Now, his time had really come.

Chen Ming passed away.

Chen Ming's cheeks were red and warm, his hands were soft and not dry, and his face showed no hardened lines; he looked relaxed and at peace, without the slightest expression of suffering. I looked down at his face, and whispered to him, 'I'm sorry; I should not have fought for this meal for you!'

Chen Ming's intestines had grown so thin that they could not tolerate this real food. It was too much, too rich; he couldn't adapt. It was my fault. From then on, it was decided that any critical prisoner on the brink of death who received special treatment would only receive cornmeal gruel; no more 'golden pagodas' would be given.

A single 25-watt bulb illuminated this room where these dozen or so half-dead people lay. More than an hour elapsed from the time when Chen Ming was carried back, through his eating of the wotous, his cries of pain, the perforation of his intestines and his death. During that time, except for my arising and speaking, nobody made the slightest movement in this cell block of a dozen or so men. To them, it was as if everything were happening on a distant planet.

I did not call the duty prisoner. I got up and knelt next to Chen Ming, and said a silent prayer asking for God's compassion.

One by one, I began to recall the dreams that Chen Ming had described to me. Those ordinary, simple dreams; those dreams that anyone who was alive would have. Was he still weaving new dreams? No, all of his dreams were in the past. He had already arrived in the true dreamland. His life was over. He had departed, and the dreams had ended.

Wherein lay the value of Chen Ming's life? What was all of this about? One hurriedly arrived in the world, and then left the world in this unfathomable manner. It was like the flame of an oil lamp that could be extinguished with one puff of breath.

Chen Ming lay there, peaceful and quiet. Nothing in the world existed for him any longer. There was no more suffering or happiness, no more dignity or humiliation, no more love or hatred. He was now a true king. I envied him.

For what purpose could such a nonsensical force exist in the world, a force that was able to extinguish the lives of so many innocents?

Translated by Bernard F. Cleary for the Laogai Research Foundation, Washington, DC, 2003

Chris Abani

Chris Abani was a political prisoner in Nigeria between 1985 and 1991 (also see p. 79). Chris's poems provide a harrowing description of his prison experiences and the torture he suffered. They were first published in a collection entitled *Kalakuta Republic*, published by Saqi Books in 2000.

Mango Chutney

Plucking mangoes
Sport for guards, soldiers, policemen.

Drunk, home-bound from shift-end
they stop at death row, choose casually,

lining us up against the wall scarred from
previous plucking, under that spreading tree.

Picking his teeth, Hassan, veteran of this
game, picks us off, shooting blindfolded.

Last rites, an unceremonious smoke
harsh, throat and lung burning.

Usually pure marijuana soaked in valium.
They aren't too good at moving targets.

Sometimes they tie us, binding to post.
Legs have a habit of giving out in the face of death,

knees kneading your shame into dust, your feet
muffling whimpers in the sand.

Tied there, you die in clockwork regularity
long before any shots are fired.

Guns spit, arcs of fire hit bodies,
jerking limbs drown in empty spaces.

Bullets dust your body apologetically; you slump
but hemp hugs tightly so only your head lolls

face hidden. Ropes cut fresh tribal marks onto
your body, weight pulling against them.

United, you crumble slowly to the floor, and leaves
fall in spirals to land on bloody corpses.

I never get used to the amount of
blood; bodies drop like so many flowers.

Eyes stare, bright and alive, into
another world. And death becomes some men.

Others wear it shamefully; others still, defiantly,
Their protest choking, suffocating.

Looking on, you notice small details.
His trousers are torn at the groin. He has a

lazy eye which gazes crookedly
into your mind.

His crime? Maybe he said no in the face of tyranny.
Maybe he murdered. The point? We will never know.

Walking over to the bodies, Hassan kicks them
hoping perhaps that they are not all dead.

The problem with mango plucking is the fruit
falls too quickly; and harvest season is over far too
     soon.

Spitting he bends down and cuts their throats
- to make doubly sure – vermin are tough and
cunning.

Judge, jury, executioner – Hassan, drunken
petty tyrant; lust rude and unbridled

by gun and 27 allocated rounds of ammo per week.
And for me a simple lust – to live as long as I can.

'Let's go,' he shouts to his friends; amid
much laughter and back slapping they leave.

'Who did they shoot tonight?' a cell mate asks.
'I don't care,' I reply looking away, 'as long as it's not
    me.'

Daily epiphanies bloom as angels walk among us,
the few, the chosen.

Section Three

EXILE

Fleeing their country of origin brings writers face to face with the problems of asylum and exile: the shock of detention and the asylum process, the brutality of racism, the difficulties of adaptation to an unfamiliar culture and climate. As the Yemeni poet Mansur Rajih writes, 'In the embrace of a strange woman, cold is our third partner.' For some the pain of exile never goes away; others find ways of forging a new identity melded from the old and the new.

Gai Tho

Gai Tho is a Tibetan poet who fled his country and now lives in India. He has published poems and articles about Tibetan culture in Tibetan, Chinese and English magazines, and has translated stories from English into Tibetan. Tao is also an editor and publishes a popular quarterly literary magazine. He remains in India and is an executive member of the Tibetan Writers Abroad Centre of PEN.

In the following poem he reflects on his exile.

Once I had a home

Once I had a home
A paradise called Sun City Lhasa
Once I knew a peaceful moon and blue sky
My home is like an ocean of peace in their eyes
Once I had a home

My home is the tears for the torn tents of the red
    ravage
Now, the yak boys, buttermilk, fled.
Plucked from their land like green corn
Are golden flames of fury.
They have become the dispossessed
lost not nomads.
They tramp listless
Fruitless farmers

Sunrise and sunset
Year after year
The fields of green turn yellow to green again

But! My home is brooding, blood-red, the tears of
Yalong River
My home a mother's mourning, Oh! Potala!
My home is her love from across the frontier.

My home is prison and a death sentence.
My home is jail.

What did I know of rights and freedom?
I don't want to know
Just one thing, look
give me back my life again
please.
One lifetime to live as I please
Whether it's old age or disease
in a peaceful world

Translated by the author

Raúl Rivero

Raúl Rivero is a Cuban poet and a former director of *CubaPress*. He was one of seventy-five dissidents arrested in a government crackdown in March 2003, accused of being financed and directed by the US Interests Section in Havana, and was sentenced under draconian laws. Rivero was freed on 30 November 2004 after having been transferred from prison to a military hospital in the capital, Havana, for medical tests. He had served twenty months of a twenty-year sentence for 'acting against Cuban independence and attempting to divide Cuban territorial unity' and for writing 'against the government', amongst other charges. He currently lives in exile in Spain, where he continues to write.

The following is one of Rivero's poems.

Family picture in Havana

Mom and I are alone once again
the same as it was at the end of the forties.

Alone, in a house that's not our own,
we tell each other last night's dreams
(in hers two old people are always crying;
in mine I've just missed a train, a plane or maybe a
        horse-drawn carriage).

Alone, my mother and I
bereft of Dad's protection, who did not, is not and
    won't ever come back
and then too because her youngest son lives in another
    country
and my oldest daughter has also left.

Mom and I, in the nineties,
at the turn of the century
again alone, we face each other,
without asking how life will be,
just really filling in the details of how it used to be.

Translated by Diana Alvarez-Amell

The following is an edited extract from Rivero's book Pruebas de contacto.

After you, God

The three Chinese Everready bicycles were on the road to Ullao, and each one carried two men. Of the six of them, three would return to the city later. The others, Luis, Gaspar and Alberto, were going to risk their lives to reach American land, on the military base of Caimanera.

Thirty kilometres from Guantánamo, in an unnamed place they had picked beforehand after canvassing the area nine times, they said goodbye. It was well into the night already, past eight o'clock. The moon was full and bright, fixed in the sky.

Luis, Gaspar and Alberto were carrying twelve 'McCastro' burgers – what Cubans maliciously call the rancid-tasting patty, made of pork and soy and shaped like a meatball – three bottles of lemonade and the inner tube of a motorcycle tyre. With these provisions, they entered the wilderness.

They walked until four in the morning, when the moon had sunk and left everything in darkness. They slept on the grass and woke early. It was Sunday, 3 December 1995, and although it was officially winter in Cuba, a powerful red sun was rising up from Maisi Point.

They had some of the burgers and a few sips of lemonade for breakfast, on a hill full of thorny shrubs and rocks from where they could see the soldiers moving at the Cuban post.

They dozed and talked about their friends and family and the holidays in Guantánamo, as if it already belonged to the past. Luis was afraid the memories of his wife's face would blur, when he recalled their first meetings in the little park and Camilo's ceramics workshop.

They were waiting to complete the final leg of their journey towards the coast. The moon returned early and lit up the cloudless sky.

In the dangerous jump down to the small shore of reefs and turbid sand, Alberto almost fell and killed himself. Around ten, they reached the coast, where a strong sea was awaiting them. They finished their food before wading into the water.

Alberto looked back towards where he imagined the rest of Cuba to be: Guantánamo, Santiago, Camagüey, Santa Clara, Matanzas and Havana, and said, 'There I leave you, communism.' Gaspar had cramps. Luis entered praying.

Alberto didn't know how to swim and clung to the smaller innertube. Gaspar flailed his arms unceremoniously, but kept afloat. Luis, little by little, was taking over the rubber ring as Alberto started complaining and becoming delirious.

Two hours later, Luis realized that the sea was returning them to the same spot. Alberto was whimpering and lying breathless on the ring. They would have to swim back to land.

Luis chose a spot where he imagined the Cuban coast was closest and started swimming towards it as he pushed Alberto. 'God, give me the strength to save this man,' Luis thought. 'Give me the strength and the serenity.'

Since the sea was turbulent and he couldn't see the coastline very well, Luis was frightened that a wave would throw them onto the jagged rocks. But right away he felt himself being lifted by bitter, smooth froth. When he came to, the three of them were on firm ground. Alberto was semi-conscious and mute. Gaspar, spent and covered with small cuts. Luis felt a sharp pain in his left foot. Around his ankle, he felt a deep, moist wound that burned like a grill.

Monday, 4 December, and the trio were on Cuba's coast again. With the sun in front of him, on his knees on the rough rocks, Luis knew he was just fifty metres from the Cuban guards' watchtower. 'We're prisoners, oh God, we're prisoners,' he said.

Convinced that his two friends wouldn't make it to the American military base, he suggested Gaspar take Alberto out to the road and return to Guantánamo. He felt spirited enough to try it again. Or they could call the guards over and turn themselves in. But Alberto refused.

They decided to hide and wait for nightfall. They had a whole day ahead of them with no water or food.

Luis, who had the small inner tube, hid it among some leaves close to where he buried himself under slates of stone and sand.

An unknown voice, strong and authoritarian, woke him from sleep. 'García, go get the rifles. I've got two sons of bitches here.' Then he heard Gaspar: 'What do you need rifles for when there are about forty of you and two of us?'

Luis watched the scene from his hiding spot. He could see military boots going to and fro, but the rest was left to his imagination. Until, just two metres in front of him, he saw them walk past in a line, en route to the border patrol, the guards' boots like part of a parade, interrupted by Alberto and Gaspar's dirty, bare and injured feet.

Luis remained hidden all day. He waited until the watch-tower's searchlight came on so that he could place where the Cubans were. When they turned it off, Luis came out of his hole, picked up the innertube and walked towards the sea.

It was calm, that night the sea was very calm, with white clouds obscuring the moon.

'Well, God, after you,' Luis said.

In the water, he felt his hands freeze, his chest hurt and he felt shaky and dizzy. Suddenly he was in his house in Guantánamo and about to lie down in his bed. Caritina was saying, 'Don't fall asleep, Luis, eat something, don't fall asleep, eat something.'

'I'm delirious, I'm crazy,' he thought and started to swim to the shore.

It started to rain, one of those tropical rainstorms, and Luis, turning and opening his mouth, felt calmed and strengthened. That's how he got to land. In front of him, a crab sat on a big, firm stone half hidden by the mist. Luis hit it with a piece of wood. He hit it hard three times and started to grind it. He felt comforted by the bitter, gelatinous substance.

He found a dry place and lay down to sleep.

On Tuesday, 5 December, Luis realized he had slept 200 metres away from a Cuban guard post. In broad daylight, he returned to the sea. He swam directly at the American military base, or at least towards where he thought the base was.

He swam rhythmically, in pain and a little confused. He couldn't see anything on the coast because of a promontory extending into the sea. He swam forcefully to pass this sliver of land and saw the US military watchtower. Then he was swimming painlessly, tirelessly, as if he were twenty years old and was bathing in the Guaso River, in Guantánamo. He swam weightlessly until he could read the tiles on the military shack's walls which announced in big white letters, 'Welcome. You've reached the land of liberty.'

Three American soldiers helped Luis climb out of the water. They handcuffed him face down on the truck's floor and drove him to an immigration office on the base.

The US authorities gave him a change of clothing (shorts, T-shirt and underwear). They tended to his wounds in the hospital. He spent fourteen days waiting for the decision that 'had to come from Washington'.

On 18 December, at six in the morning, an official appeared at the camp where Luis was detained along with twenty other Cubans and told him that in two hours he would be returning to Cuba because his application for asylum hadn't been approved.

The immigration agreements between Cuba and the US, signed 12 May 1995, stipulate the return to the island of anyone who tries to illegally enter American territory and cannot prove that he would be at risk of going to jail in his own country.

Two hours after the official's visit, Luis picked up a small bag with deodorant, soap and some razors and was driven to the border along with three compatriots, two from Santiago and one from Villa Clara. There, he was given a document that would allow him to enter the US Interests Section in Cuba, so that he could start the process to immigrate legally. At eight in the morning, sixteen days after leaving Guantánamo by bicycle with Alberto and Gaspar, Luis Sánchez Díaz, forty-one years old, construction technician, former member of the Union of Young Communists, Jehovah's Witness, and father of two children, walked towards a white line. On the other side of the painted line was his homeland.

When he made his first step back into Cuba, a policeman

came up to him and said in his ear, 'Walk next to me, gaze forward, and be careful about making any gestures.'

'That's how I knew I was in my country,' Luis tells me on an April morning, in Havana, 1997.

'I felt something sharp inside suffocating me, because I couldn't understand how I could risk my life so many times to reach my friends, and then they turned me back to the enemy.'

Translated by Anna Kushner

Jean-Louis Ntadi

Jean-Louis Ntadi, a playwright, political activist with the main opposition party and Red Cross humanitarian worker, was born in 1964 in Congo-Brazzaville. Ntadi was persecuted by the government in the Republic of Congo following the staging of his play *Le Chef de l'État*, a parable highly critical of the presidency of Sassou-Nguesso, performed in January 2001. The play was forcibly closed and banned throughout the Republic of Congo.

Ntadi went into hiding, obtaining a visa for the UK in December 2003. Arriving at Heathrow Airport in February 2004, he was refused asylum in the UK. Ntadi passed through five detention centres and endured countless interviews and humiliations. He was finally detained at Campsfield House immigration detention centre, before being released on bail. After pressure from PEN he was allowed to make a fresh claim for asylum.

This is an edited version of Ntadi's twenty-minute play Cries of the Cricket, *based on his experiences of applying for asylum, while in detention in the UK. It was staged on the London Eye and at the National Theatre in June 2005.*

Cries of the cricket

Man: You are accused of using a false passport to come to the UK.

Youwane: If you are in a house that is burning, do you break a window to get out or do you die in the house because the main door is locked?

Man: You have been asked a question, Mr Youwane. Did you have the right to use the passport you used?

Youwane: No, because it was for priority people. Yes, because I had to flee danger and death. If I asked you to choose between a passport and a life, which would you want to choose?

Man: You are accused of being violent. What can you say about this?

Youwane: What is this violence which I am said to have practised? Yes, I refused to be returned to my country, where I am in danger of death. But believe me, your prosecution is like the thief that cries 'thief'.

He leaves the trial and directly addresses the audience.

My name is Youwane. I am here in England, alone. They want to deport me to a place where I will be killed. Back home my wife and six children are constantly harassed by the police who are determined to track me down. I'm frightened about what they will do to my wife. They might rape her. They might kill her. The family move from village to village to escape the danger. They are now in an area where the police cannot reach them. There is civil war and no telephone communications.

So they are still in danger but now I have no contact. Only in my dreams.

His wife appears in a dream.

Soso: We gaze at the home you built, fearing that death might take us by surprise if we stay.

Youwane: Yes, my love. It is the politics of the lion. Where the lion is king no animal is allowed to lie beside him.

Soso: Villages, districts, whole regions have been pillaged by the authorities corrupted by the folly of Black Gold …

Youwane: Children of ten or twelve are armed to the teeth.

Soso: The politics of the lion.

Youwane: This greed will destroy Africa. The strong never share the wealth of the country with others.

Soso: This greed is now on such a scale. We eat petrol. We drink petrol, we dress ourselves in petrol, we dance petrol. It's petrol a go-go.

Youwane: Our country has been taken hostage. Giant ants have invaded all the avenues, even the smaller streets of our nation; so we must pull back in order to move forward again.

Soso: Sooner or later we will see each other so it is worth weeping. It's better to seek the protection of the Queen of England, who knows a little of the reality of African politics, and who knows more still about human rights and fundamental liberties.

Youwane: I am merely fleeing this rain which seems to carry all before it; but the moment that it ends I will return. The rain will cease, the sky will chase away the bad clouds, and then the day will dawn again. And God will bless us a hundredfold for what we have lost.

Soso: One thing I ask you, husband, is that you are not harassed by the beautiful women of Queen Elizabeth. May God be with you and stay with you during your exile in the country of the Queen.

Back to the interrogation

Man: Do you know where you are, sir?

Youwane: I am in the country of Queen Elizabeth. I am in the UK.

Man: What is the reason for your visit to the UK?

Youwane: I was persecuted in my country; that's why I am here.

Man: Your profession, please, sir.

Youwane: Teacher, artist, writer, first-aid worker.

Man: So many ... And are you married, sir?

Youwane: I am married and the father of six children.

Man: Do you have brothers, friends, families or other contacts in the UK?

Youwane: No. I have no close relations here despite the fact that I have sought refuge here.

Man: Refuge? On what basis have you been persecuted? On political grounds, or for other reasons?

Youwane: I was persecuted as a member of the opposition party. I denounced the evil of the authorities and the way they treated our people. I wrote a play which has created trouble for me.

Man: I believe your government came to power through an election, Mr Youwane?

Youwane: We are very far from the reality of democracy. What flourishes in my country is dictatorship, egoism, greed, anarchy, the crushing of the people, torture, killing, pillage, rape, debauchery and xenophobia.

Soso: Despite all this your country is still populated.

Youwane: Yes. Not everyone is targeted. Only those who speak out. But please understand, sir, those who suffer most are the innocent, the people.

Man: Do you suffer from any specific illness?

Youwane: I get chronic fevers and suffer from impaired vision and low blood pressure – all from the torture I was subjected to back home.

Man: You will be taken from here to prison.

Youwane: To prison? As an asylum seeker?

Man: I mean to a detention centre where your case will be dealt with in two or three days.

Change.

Man: Are you a terrorist?

Soso: A rapist?

Man: A thief? An assassin?

Soso: Do you organize coups?

Youwane: I am an artist, a writer. What I have written has angered the government and because of this I have been the victim of evil right until the moment of my arrival in England.

Man: Are you telling me the truth and nothing but the truth?

Youwane: Again. Here is my story. I was persecuted in my country, imprisoned for fourteen months, tortured and had my house regularly searched. My life was in danger. I had to flee. A search warrant was posted to find me.

Man: But you also say you are a teacher. And sometimes an orderly for the Red Cross. Next you're a politician. And all the while an artist, a writer, a dramatist. What are we supposed to make of all that?

Youwane: Quite simply, since I am a graduate in dramatic art I write books; but I also work for the Red Cross as a medical orderly and I am a member of a political party. And I help to teach the young to read and write.

Man: What is the name of your party?

Youwane: The Movement for Democracy, the main opposition party whose president is also in exile.

Man: You did not follow your president to the country he went to? Correct?

Youwane: When a violent wind hits a piles of leaves stacked in a corner, the leaves do not always fly away in the same direction.

Man: Are you against authority or simply against the present government in power?

Youwane: I could not possibly be against democracy. I am against those who are pillaging my country. Against those who believe in the one-party state.

Man: What can you say for yourself as a dramatist, Mr Youwane?

Youwane: My play could have cost me my life.

Man: What did the authorities dislike about this play?

Youwane: Firstly, its style; secondly, its content. I was accused of libel, of being desperate for power, selling secret information, dissidence, other things. Is it normal for an exile to be put in prison as soon as he arrives here?

Man: What is the play's message?

Youwane: Its main message is social justice. That power must no longer come out of a gun. That money from our oil is for the people, not for one group.

Man: Your request for asylum ... Is it based on being a writer? A Red Cross orderly or being a politician?

Youwane: I was persecuted on the grounds of all three.

Soso: How long do you want to stay in the UK?

Youwane: Until the mortar shells stop raining on my country.

Soso: Are you tired, Youwane?

Youwane: Of course, and I fear I will be so for days and weeks to come.

Man: As I told you at the beginning you are in the fast-track system and everything is being done quickly. After your initial interviews, the Immigration Office refused your asylum application to the UK. We are not convinced about your nationality.

Youwane: So what nationality do they think I have?

Man: Don't panic, Mr Youwane. You can appeal against it. Also you have too many professions and they are unable to decide which is the real one.

Soso: Thirdly, you have neither family nor friends in the UK.

Man: Fourthly, your travel documents are not in order. In addition, you have too many children.

Youwane: How can you blame me for having too many children?

Man: This review is finished. You have to remain in prison to await the course of any judicial review.

Time shift

Soso: You have been taken to the airport four times to be deported and on one of these occasions you were beaten up by your guards. Can't you go home quietly and avoid these humiliations and dishonour?

Youwane: Have you ever seen a corpse who fears decomposition? Or a body submerged by water which is afraid of being soaked?

Man: I think you must consider carefully before it is too late.

Youwane: Here a foreigner always remains a foreigner. I don't think of anyone in this world as 'illegal'. Don't think coming to the UK is for me a luxury or an honour. It was simply a necessity. I'm not trying to invade your land.

Man: Well, if your life really is in danger back home, then living in prison here is better than that, is it not?

Woman: Tomorrow is the hearing to decide whether Mr Youwane should be released.

Man: There is no proper evidence to justify his release.

Woman: In your opinion how long should someone spend in detention?

Man: There is no limit, in my opinion.

Woman: Does not the length of detention depend on the development of the person's dossier? Mr Youwane has spent fourteen months in detention. Does that have no moral significance for you? Why not release him first and see how his situation develops?

Man: Release him to what address? Youwane has no friends or family in the UK.

Woman: This is not a fair argument.

Man: We don't even know his nationality. This man whom you wish to release is violent. When he was being sent back to his country he lashed out at his escorts.

Woman: Do you have evidence of this violence?

Man: The escort in question resigned his post after the incident.

Woman: Can we invite the escort to give evidence about the incident to this court, bringing with him a medical certificate?

Man: Since he is no longer in service it would be extremely difficult to see him, even to call him.

Man: You were persecuted for your play. What did you say in it?

Youwane: That the President must be merciful to his people.

Man: And then?

Youwane: That power must no longer come out of a gun. That nobody should be exiled even if his thoughts differ from others' or if he is against the ruling power. There should be no more sacrifices of people to defend the state. Money from our oil is for the people, not for one ethnic group, one clan, or one political class of dictators. I want to see dialogue, a round table, social justice, peace, brotherhood and national unity as the basis of true democracy. Tribal and ethnic hatreds, anger, the settling of accounts, the violation of laws and rights must disappear in the hearts of our leaders. Precisely, because in my country people are begging for help, are escaping and seeking asylum all the time.

Man: Thank you, Mr Youwane. The court has considered

everything you have to say. For having deceived the government, used violence and false documents, I believe this court should reject your application. Have you anything to say?

Youwane: What I want to say is that you only have one life. If you lose it you are finished. You are dead. When it is in danger it must be saved, protected as it is by UN articles and by divine law. Life must not be separate from freedom because freedom is the very wealth of life. Depriving a life of liberty is a crime against humanity and against God. This is my final word.

Man: We have listened with close attention to the arguments of both parties. After analysing all the documents we, an independent immigration court, have decided as follows: We understand that Mr Youwane used false documents to enter the UK.

Woman: We understand that he has not sought asylum elsewhere.

Man: That he entered the UK without a valid visa. That he has not spoken the truth before the law.

Woman: That he has no family or contacts in the UK.

Man: That certain members of his political party have remained in the country and continue to operate.

Woman: That his country continues to function normally despite coups and civil wars.

Man: That his country's president was voted into office with 99.99 per cent of the popular vote.

Woman: That opposition exists in his country despite the fact that its leaders are in exile.

Man: In the light of all this the court has decided to refuse to release Mr Youwane or to give him asylum in this country. You have a final chance to make a second appeal within forty-eight hours. Please bring proof of your employment as an orderly with the Red Cross, as evidence that will help us believe in you a little. The hearing is over.

Back to Youwane's dream.

Soso: Sooner or later we will see each other so it is worth weeping. It's better to seek the protection of the Queen of England, who knows a little of the reality of African politics, and who knows more still about human rights and fundamental liberties.

Youwane: I am merely fleeing this rain which seems to carry all before it; but the moment that it ends I will return. The rain will cease, the sky will chase away the bad clouds, and then the day will dawn again. And God will bless us a hundredfold for what we have lost.

[END]

Translated by Trevor Mostyn and developed by Ben Jancovich

Mansur Muhammad Ahmad Rajih

Mansur Muhammad Ahmad Rajih is a Yemeni writer and poet who was arrested in January 1983, on his return from Lebanon, where he had been a university student. He was initially held for six months without trial, and then released before being rearrested eight days later. He was tried in March 1984 for the murder of a man from his village and was given the death penalty. The evidence was regarded as spurious, the trial was rife with irregularities, and witnesses were not able to identify Rajih as a suspect. PEN believed the evidence against the poet was fabricated and that he was held because of his political activities as a student in Libya and then Lebanon. Rajih reported that he had been tortured and forced to make a confession.

Following an international campaign led by Norwegian PEN, Rajih was released, on 7 February 1998, after fifteen years in prison.

Aided by Norwegian PEN, Rajih currently lives with his wife in Stavanger, Norway and the following are poems he has written about his exile and time in prison.

Another sky

An asphalt sky: your memory
Your earth is only a body
Time is a poem approaching
Time is a poem withering

Time is a poem dying
& time is a waiting wall
for poems and dreams

Such is exile
Your bottlenecked bottleneck
The wounded Fatherland's open sores
moaning within you

An asphalt sky: your memory
Your earth is only a body

For San'a

She is present like
Waves within my soul
She is a citizen of my heart
Authorized to reside in my voice
All I know is born of San'a's longing
My body has been formed of her body
Why then is her name not 'I'?
The stuff of my consciousness
Is from within her
Is from her
Stronger

The soul alone

The street is deserted – no one
It's cold – no one
In the evening, you long for morning
In the morning, you rush from under the heavy duvet.

News from the homeland
unsettles you
(had you the energy to become unsettled)
The wells of hope are dry
The past is jammed in your throat
Images of a future – have gone with your fractured
      memories

This is exile. You don't know.
Perhaps we create an identity unique for this climate?
Perhaps it is the homeland that
reaches into the soul of the exile
this morning –
chokes him.

This morning has gone
just like all the cold mornings in exile –

Alone

Eiganes[1]

Here, in this quiet, the trees are proud of themselves
Longing eats at the heart
There is no life in exile
Here, the sound has no echo
The poem flees from between your hands,
flees to the heat of Yemen
Love is blocked by questions
What does get through is strangled by frost
A new morning over you, the silent city

---

1 A neighbourhood in Stavanger, Norway.

Pain wars pain within the heart
This stretch of time eats at the mind

The wind brings nothing to the banished man,
and leaving, it carries nothing hence[2]

Contradictions

I don't have enough reason
to die
So why should I die?

I don't have enough time
to live
So why should I live?

Here I am dead
To live
in the poem

It's not easy to break me

I am not broken
For you, I would not allow myself to break
I have not collapsed in shame before your eyes
Your eyes ignited
the flame of defiance within me
It means you are here

I would not moan, for you would hear me
I sang

---

2 An Arab proverb.

with all my passion
so that you would dance for me
I sensed your steps, following,
hearing the movements
of your breasts:
A sound
that merged with my song
Echoes of song
undulating between us
Your sweating body dancing
exuding a fragrance
which healed the eternity of disease within me
I burrowed deeply into my song –
into you

Prison cannot contain me
A sentence cannot limit me

Because I live in you
nothing can break me

Stranger

Strange, in a strange city
near the North Sea
Strange in the embrace of a strange woman
Cold is our third partner
And the question
Strange, in a strange soul
Strange to itself
Standing before words
I don't understand

A situation that is difficult to comprehend
Thus –
Past: Sorrow
Present: Oh
The future comes into view
like a cloud in the horizon of travel
and I am strange, like the impossible

Translated by Ren Powell and Mansur Rajih

Cheikh Kone

The journalist Cheikh Kone fled the Ivory Coast in October 2000 to avoid harassment from the government following his article criticizing the presidential elections. After a circuitous journey, he arrived in Fremantle, Australia, where he was taken into a holding centre for asylum seekers. He remained in detention, while his case was under consideration, until July 2003. Australian PEN centres vigorously campaigned for his release. He now lives in Canberra, where he works for the Community and Public Sector Union.

Here is an edited account of his seeking asylum in Australia.

The long road

I was brought up in a country without democracy, like so many in the world. But like so many in the world democracy was what I believed in. As a student protesting against one-party rule in that country, the Ivory Coast, democracy seemed the way of a brighter, better future. It was my own belief in democracy that led me to criticize my government.

On 26 October 2000 I was forced to leave my beloved homeland because I had written an article which underlined the manipulation of the result of the presidential election that same year. I fled first across the border into Ghana, travelling by road but hidden. From Ghana I made my way to Togo and then on into Benin. There I was put on a container ship I hoped would take me to Europe, but which instead deposited me in South Africa.

After spending the longest six weeks of my life in a South African port scraping a living, I stowed away in another freighter without knowing where it was bound. After eight days and nine nights without food or water, my companion from Sierra Leone and I were discovered in the engine room by the sailors. We feared for our lives, but the Italian sailors looked after us well and told us that the vessel was headed for Belgium and that in three days we would be in Brussels.

The following morning, the vessel docked in Fremantle. One night passed and nothing happened. But early the next day I was woken and told someone wanted to speak to me. I was rushed to another room where I believed I was going to be welcomed to Australia. Instead, two very hostile individuals confronted me without introduction. With my poor English I was able to comprehend some of what they were saying. Who had told me to come to Australia? Didn't I know that coming to Australia this way was harshly punishable? In return I told them that I was a journalist who had been forced to leave the Ivory Coast because my writings had annoyed the government of the day.

They interviewed me for hours. One of them told me I was a liar and I was going to be repatriated in the next couple of hours. Eventually they took me back to the cabin I had been sleeping in, where I was first body-searched by customs officers and then locked up. The following day I was transferred to the Immigration Detention Centre in Perth. After a night there I was flown to Port Hedland.

Entering Port Hedland that sunny Australian morning, the temperature was over fifty degrees. Once the plane had landed, I was put in a van and driven for about twenty minutes. The vehicle stopped in front of a huge steel gate: on the side of it a sign read 'Immigration Reception and Processing Centre'.

The entrance to the Centre looked like the gates of a prison. Confused, I asked one of the officers with me if we were being detained. He said, 'No.' Then the gate opened and the van entered. As I got out of the van my first impression was that the place seemed like a jail despite the officer's words. All I could see was an endless barbed-wire fence. I was handed over to another officer and led away.

Inside the Centre they searched my arms, my legs, my groin, roughly. Then they put me in a small room with cameras for several hours. By now I was convinced I had been jailed and that I was a prisoner of Australia, a place I had always thought so friendly, with athletes like Cathy Freeman from the 2000 Olympic Games. When night fell I was transferred to another building. I was to spend almost two weeks there. To use the toilet I had to wait for hours; I was not allowed to use a phone, to watch television or even to use a pen. I was only allowed outside into the fresh air for one hour every twenty-four.

After two weeks I was moved to another location. Here I met an interpreter and a solicitor. At first I thought they were people to trust, who would help me, but once they started asking me questions they began to challenge my story. I got the impression they too thought I was lying. One said, 'You'll have a hard time here being an African, especially an intelligent African; you're not welcome in Australia.' They twisted the story I told them, pounding me psychologically and telling me DIMIA's [Department of Immigration and Multicultural and Indigenous Affairs] officers would not believe me until at last I stopped talking. They told me again DIMIA would not believe me and then called a guard to take me away.

A week later I was interviewed by the immigration officer. This interview was even worse. He questioned everything I said and constantly put me down. 'So you think you're intelligent?' he demanded. I said again and again that I had rights, that this is not the way people should be treated. He told me these so-called rights would be my downfall in this process. When at last this torture ended, I was taken to an open compound where I was left with many others and a multitude of nationalities. A week later I was refused refugee status.

I spent another two and a half years in the Centre. We were treated like children, every aspect of our lives controlled. First they gave us identification numbers. Suddenly I was no longer Cheikh Kone but NBP451. Every morning at 6 a.m. they woke us and made us line up for a head count before breakfast. This was a very regimented process. Everyone had to have breakfast between 7 a.m. and 9 a.m. People who were sick or couldn't come got nothing. There were more head counts. First at lunch and then at midnight. Even the children had to wake up for this. Then at 3 a.m. they had another: depending on how you look at it the last or the first of the day. Once again we all had to wake up and call out our numbers. If the officers could not find a particular person, everybody had to stay where they were, as if we were playing a game of 'freeze' with no moving whatsoever. Gates were locked, all cameras were checked, officers were on alert watching anyone who moved until the missing number was found. These lockdowns could last three to six hours; children were expected to stand still and if a mealtime coincided with the lockdown it was postponed.

But it was the nights that were the worst. Before I was sent there I only had nightmares while I slept; there we had nightmares while awake. The screaming and yelling was constant and never seemed to stop. People would run by in the corridors, their footsteps so loud you could not shut them out and the officers' radios never seemed to stop, no matter how far away they were from the rooms. Over time I saw inmates mutilating themselves and sewing their lips together. I saw one man attempt suicide by climbing a tree and jumping head first out of it. Before he jumped he shouted, 'I don't want Australia any more, thank you, Australia, thank you, everybody.' He didn't die but he ended up in hospital for quite some time. When he came back his spirit seemed to have left him and he stopped talking or even interacting with the rest of us. I never saw him smile again after that day. In the end he was deported. There was so much pain – suicide attempts, constant crying, shouting, the rules, the unpredictable lockdowns – that even now, three years later, sitting in my rented unit with a regular job and my girlfriend on her way home from work, I find it hard to type. Just thinking about it brings back such horrible memories, so much hurt that as I type the tears are coming, the hope I hung on to disappearing when I remember seeing people I had befriended doing things I would never imagine human beings capable of. I can't write any more, it hurts too much but I refuse to let my heart be hardened by it and so I make myself let it go …

Throughout my detention, I asked myself many questions. Why are we treated like this? Was it a crime to seek asylum in Australia? After moving into the main compound we began to receive newspapers, listen to the radio and watch television. Every day there was a story about refugees invading Australia. It became clear to me that the decision makers in Australia had developed a lexicon of demeaning rhetoric especially for refugees and that the media conspired in this until mainstream Australia had come to believe we were all criminals and terrorists, invading this great brown land of theirs.

About halfway through my detention I was so dismayed by the conditions in the Centre that I asked to start a newsletter. After several rejections I was allowed to, as long as the things I wrote and published were not political. But despite promising to follow these guidelines I could not stop myself from criticizing the Centre's administration and the Federal government. And so after two issues the Centre's management stopped it, saying my articles were too gloomy. But this didn't stop me writing. The walls of my room, its doors were enough inspiration for me to write, write and never stop writing. And once I started writing my story down I found the strength to refuse to let them call me by my number or carry my card, and once I had done that others began to do the same.

After many months in detention, I met Peter Job and his partner April Weiss through a letter-writing scheme initiated by Rural Australians for Refugees. When I phoned them the response was unexpected; they made me feel welcome. I told them my story. From that time on Peter and I began a long-distance friendship. He took on my case and mentioned it to someone from a human rights group, who suggested that he contact International PEN. The Head Office in London investigated my case and established that the story I had told DIMIA was true. PEN forwarded a letter of concern to the Prime Minister of Australia about their findings.

With the help of people like the refugee advocate Naleya Everson and many others, Peter began to compile a detailed submission to the Minister for Immigration on PEN's behalf. He submitted it in November 2002. For a long time nothing happened, but finally in early April 2003 the Minister replied that he had decided to intervene on my behalf, subject to legal and health checks. I was elated of course, throughout the two months it took for the legal checks to come back from South Africa. Two more months were to elapse before I was finally free.

The frustration and despair I felt in the final few months of detention were the hardest. Like my first months in the Centre, when it seemed there were new lies every day, I found it harder and harder to hold on to hope. Day after day for four agonizing months I was told tomorrow, tomorrow, until at last I was almost broken, both emotionally and mentally. Then at 2 p.m.

on 29 July 2003 I was informed that the Minister of Immigration had finally granted me freedom. I was to be given a permanent residency visa and released. In a split second my life was changed. Even when they told me I had fifteen minutes to pack my things it still seemed like a dream. I was thrilled my visa would let me come and go as I pleased, do what I wanted when I wanted, live where I wanted – things we take for granted.

After my release, I received a tax invoice from the Immigration Department for $89,000 for the costs of my detention. At first I thought it was a joke, so I rang the financial branch of DIMIA. They told me that there was no mistake and that I had to pay. A month or two before I was sent the invoice, I received an invitation to speak at International PEN's Congress in Barcelona. I was excited to be given an opportunity to speak about my experience at an international level and had assumed there would be no problem with attending because I had a permanent resident visa and PEN had offered to cover my expenses. When I received the invoice I still thought it would be OK and went ahead and applied for the necessary documents, only for them to be denied at the last moment because of an 'administrative error'.

Between adolescence and adulthood a political ideal called democracy caught my attention. Amidst the mosaic of ideas that offered themselves I quickly became an advocate of this ideal, believing in its great strengths. After spending almost three years in an immigration detention centre in a so-called democratic country, I don't know what to believe in any more.

Taslima Nasrin

Taslima Nasrin has written poetry, essays, novels and short stories in her native language of Bengali. She was forced to leave Bangladesh in 1994 after receiving death threats from Islamic fundamentalists and being charged with blasphemy. In 1998, however, she managed to gain permission to return and visit her ailing mother, who died on 11 January 1999. Two weeks later, Nasrin was forced to flee once more, after receiving another round of death threats. Today, she continues to live in exile.

The following is an extract from a poem she wrote about her mother's death

Mother

None doubted that she would go to Paradise,
would walk hand in hand with Mohammed
on a lovely afternoon, soon, in a garden.
The two would lunch – bird meat, wine.

Mother dreamed her lifelong dream:
she would walk with Mohammed
in the Garden of Paradise.
But now,
at the very time for departing Earth,
she hesitated.

Instead of stepping outside,
she wished first
to boil Birui rice for me,
to cook fish curry and fry a whole hilsa,
to make sauce with seasonal red potatoes.
She wished to pick for me a young coconut
from the south corner of her garden.
She wished to fan me by hand,
remove a few straggly hairs from my forehead.
She wished to put a new sheet on my bed,
to sew for me a shirt with embroidery.
She wished to walk barefoot in the courtyard,
to support the young guava plant with a bamboo stick.
She wished to sing on a moonlit night.

Never before,
sitting in the garden of hasnuhena flowers,
had such a bright moon shone down.
And never before
had such feelings come over me:
her ever-maternal love,
her surprising wish to stay,
holding my warm hand.

Translated by Taslima Nasrin and Warren Allen Smith

Chenjerai Hove

Chenjerai Hove is a poet, novelist and columnist who was forced to leave Zimbabwe after suffering various forms of persecution.

Hove worked as senior literary editor in Zimbabwe for over ten years and was the founding Chairperson of the Zimbabwe Writers' Union. He worked as Regional Cultural Editor for Interpress Service (southern Africa) from 1988 to 1991 before he was appointed to the honorary post of Writer-in-Residence at the University of Zimbabwe (1991–4). The following year Hove was International Writer-in-Residence for Yorkshire and Humberside Arts, northern England.

Hove has published five poetry anthologies, four novels, four essay collections and a bilingual children's book (French and English). His award-winning novel *Bones* has been translated into several languages. He continues to travel widely, conducting lectures, public readings and writers' workshops.

This is an edited version of a talk he gave at the International PEN congress held in Tromsø, Norway in 2004.

The burdens of creativity in Africa – reflections

A Brazilian writer told a stunned audience in an international writers' conference in Rio de Janeiro that writers should not worry too much about the Ministry of Culture imposing its interpretations of culture on them. 'What we, as writers, should worry about, as a matter of grave concern, is the culture of the Minister of Culture.' Ask any African minister of culture which African novels he or she has read recently, and that is enough to earn yourself a secret agent file.

A haunted poet from West Africa told me that he was afraid of four people in his country. He feared the Minister of the Interior because the man was in charge of the police who arrest him. He feared the Minister of Justice because he made the laws under which the writer is arrested. He feared the Minister of Culture, who wants to impose his definition of culture on the writer. He feared the Minister of Information, who has the tendency to think that writers are his unpaid public relations officers.

The Italian novelist Italo Calvino once said there is a danger to literature if politicians concern themselves too much with matters literary. There was also a danger to literature if politicians show a total lack of interest in literature. The ideal, he speculated, was a healthy tension in which each respected the other's province and left it alone.

As far back as 1987 I challenged the Minister of Culture to produce his own example of what he publicly demanded writers produce: 'socialist novels and plays'. I argued that since the minister knew what these 'socialist' literary works were all about, he should go ahead and write one himself which we could use as a model. It is writers who should be in the business of telling the minister what novels it is possible to write and how to write them, not the other way round.

Ironically, the current Zimbabwe government, in power since 1980, perfected the laws of fear from colonial times. Before a writer sits down to write a poem or a book, he or she has to think whether the material is likely to endanger public security and threaten law and order. So, the burdened writer sits at home with a manuscript, afraid to take it to the publisher since publishers are required by law to submit to the secret service any creative works likely to endanger public order and security.

Not so long ago, mysterious figures broke into my house and stole my two computers (the laptop and the PC) and diskettes. When I reported the theft by phone, the police had no car to visit the scene of the crime. I drove to fetch them, but when one officer saw me, he asked if I was the writer and journalist.

'Are you sure this is not a political crime?' he asked before they left. From then on I knew there would be no investigations of the matter.

Before the thefts, I had been offered a farm on condition that I stop criticizing government policies. When I turned down the offer because it was stolen property, I was offered lots of money, which I was not obliged to account for, in order to travel the whole world persuading all PEN centres to agree to the government's invitation to host the PEN Annual Congress in Zimbabwe.

'The government's image is bad internationally. If you bring writers here, the government will pamper them so they can write good things about our country,' the government emissary had said to me. Knowing the futility of such an enterprise, I refused to take the money under the pretext that if the writers agreed to come to Zimbabwe, I could not guarantee what they were going to write about the country.

From persuasion and the lure of money, they went for other alternatives, including incessant death threats against me and my family. The most bizarre was when four armed policemen tried to arrest me at my house alleging that my car had been found abandoned in Plumtree, over 700 kilometres away, with a load of 23.5 kilos of marijuana. The numberplates were of a car which I had sold through a garage five years before.

Finally I left under the pretext that I was visiting the United Kingdom and returning after ten days. I have never returned.

Zimbabwe has been classed as one of the worst countries for the profession of journalism. Police in the country called it 'the crime of practising journalism'. Journalists in prison cells are not allowed anywhere near pen and paper.

But as a writer, a poet, a playwright, one wants to create new metaphors and symbols of our collective and individual identities. The urge to write is like the urge to live, to fight the silence that suffocates the human soul, especially in Africa. I try to write in order to fight the decay called silence, to communicate with myself so as to search for the 'other' in me.

I see my writing as defiance of the fear instilled in our society by the cruel laws as well as a ruthless police force. When I take up my pen to write, I feel the strength of standing up and refusing to be silent. No one has the right to deny me the right to describe the colours and scents of the flowers of my dignity or the lack of it. Under a dictatorship, even flowers belong to the state. Even clothes, what we want to wear, belong to the state.

An oppressive system depends on a massive programme to make all citizens imbeciles. A writer has to fight that, especially on the African continent. In the process, new symbols of our collective identity are created against those offered to us by government praise-singers and flatterers. What keeps me going is that every new word and metaphor I create is a little muscle in the act of pushing the dictatorship away from our real and imaginative existence.

When citizens are not allowed to participate in the affairs of the country in all possible ways, they are in exile. You do not have to be out of your country to be in exile. After all, the very act of creativity is an act of exile since one sits alone in a quiet corner, clinging to a vision, writing it down on paper, removed from the day-to-day activities of other mortals. Six months of total seclusion while one writes a novel, that in itself is exile. Let alone clinging to a vision which those in power refuse to see.

I remember many years ago being accused of being too critical of President Mugabe's leadership style and economic and social policies. The usual accusation was: you are being too harsh with this government. If Mugabe goes, there is no one intelligent enough to take over. To which I responded that there were over twelve million Zimbabweans capable of running the country since that is the only job for which one does not need any formal qualifications.

The writer has to survive if his or her work is to last longer than political regimes. A repressive political regime forces energetic writers to create new, visible and invisible metaphors. When repressive laws were passed, including a ban on criticizing the President, I decided to go back to the traditional folk tale as a device to fight the law. African folk tales are a massive tool and device to beat the system creatively. Like in southern Africa, there was always the praise-poet, a free spirit who was not only praising the king, but used his harsh tongue and poetic skills to chastize the king publicly. And traditionally the praise-poet was never arrested or imprisoned because most African civilizations did not have prisons.

Once upon a time, in the land of animals, the monkey used to boast about its ability to climb the tallest tree in the land. He invited other animals to join him so they could look at the beauty of the landscape from above. The Sheep, Monkey's good friend, said he would rather not venture up trees. He preferred to be on the solid ground to see and touch reality. Some animals tried to join Monkey but they could only go so far and not as high as Monkey. So, they gave up, while warning Monkey on the dangers of climbing too high.

One day Monkey found the tallest tree. His climbing skills urged him to show the rest that he was the best tree climber in the world. Refusing the warnings of the other animals to desist from the temptation to climb on, Monkey went up higher and higher and higher until he felt he could touch the sky.

All the animals were under the tree, admiring Monkey as he climbed. 'Stop! It is enough!' the other animals warned him. But he would not listen.

When he had climbed to the top of the tree, he celebrated and danced on the branches, shaking all the leaves and flowers up there. But when he looked down at where he had come from, every animal was in fits of laughter. Every one of them, including Sheep, his friend. The cows, the goats, the elephants, the lions, were all dying of laughter.

As Monkey returned to the ground, he asked why all the animals were laughing so much.

'The higher the monkey climbs, the more it exposes its bottom,' Sheep said, in between outbursts of mirth.

So it is with power of any kind, political or otherwise. The higher one ascends the tree of power, the more the public have a chance to observe and scrutinize one's political or economic bottom.

Adaptation of these innocent-looking tales, the use of provocative proverbs and other wise sayings – these are some of the devices we inherited from the ancient storytellers, which the writer in oppressive situations finds useful.

Only recently a Zimbabwean musician was in trouble for singing an innocent song which celebrates old age. The song was called 'Bvuma', meaning 'acknowledge', narrating the natural cycle of birth, maturity and old age. One has the duty and responsibility to acknowledge ageing as a natural process which is inescapable.

When the song came out, the political interpreters were sure the song referred to Mugabe. The musician was haunted by the presidential youth militia, and barred from performing publicly in one of our small towns. The song is just a celebration of ageing, it had nothing to do with any politician, the musician argued. They stopped it being aired on radio and television.

Despite the censorship of bad economic policies depriving people of the money to buy books, despite the burden of illiteracy deliberately inflicted upon people so that they are not able to read their own constitution and learn about their basic human rights, an African writer continues to write. Despite the fear instilled in the hearts of the people, an African writer continues to search for the hidden smiles which linger in the hearts of the oppressed.

The politician was elected by thousands of voters, so he says, despite the rigging, and the writer was elected by no one, so has the right to speak out against abuses which border on the bizarre. With the political madness of our continent, Africa, there is never a shortage of creative material to use in art.

Section Four

THE FREEDOM TO WRITE

Voices of conscience from around the world defend writers' freedoms in this selection of essays, lectures and speeches. Anna Politkovskaya chillingly predicts her own death. Aung San Suu Kyi discusses the relationship between power, corruption and fear. Orhan Pamuk recalls the historic PEN mission to Turkey of Arthur Miller and Harold Pinter in 1985, when Pamuk was their guide. Jiang Qisheng mourns the death of democracy in China. Hari Kunzru reports on cyber-dissidence. Ken Saro-Wiwa writes his last letter to PEN.

Anna Politkovskaya

The award-winning Russian journalist Anna Politkovskaya was murdered on 7 October 2006 and it is widely
believed that her death is linked to her fearless reporting,
particularly on the Chechen wars. She was a special
correspondent for *Novaya gazeta*, Moscow, and her writing
about Chechnya include the books *A Dirty War: A Russian
Reporter in Chechnya* (2001) and *Putin's Russia* (2004). *A
Russian Diary*, the book Anna was working on at the time of
her untimely death, is due to be published by Harvill Secker
in 2007. Politkovskaya acted as a mediator in the Nord-Ost
theatre siege in Moscow in 2002. Two years later she fell
seriously ill as she attempted to fly to Beslan to cover the
hostage crisis there, leading to speculation that she had
been deliberately poisoned to stop her from reporting on
the crisis. Politkovskaya was recognized worldwide for her
championing of human rights.

The following essay was written just weeks before her tragic death.

I am a pariah.

That is the main result of my journalism throughout the
years of the Second Chechen War, and of publishing abroad a
number of books about life in Russia and the Chechen War.
In Moscow I am not invited to press conferences or gatherings
which officials of the Kremlin Administration might attend, in
case the organizers are suspected of harbouring sympathies
towards me. Despite this, all the top officials talk to me, at my

request, when I am writing articles or conducting investigations – but only in secret, where they can't be observed, in the open air, in squares, in secret houses which we approach by different routes, like spies.

The officials like talking to me. They are happy to give me information. They consult me and tell me what is going on at the top. But only in secret.

You don't get used to this, but you learn to live with it. It is exactly the way I have had to work throughout the Second War in Chechnya. First I was hiding from the Russian federal troops, but was always able to make contact clandestinely with individuals through trusted intermediaries, so that my inform-ants would not be denounced to the top generals. When Putin's plan of Chechenization succeeded (setting 'good' Chechens loyal to the Kremlin to killing 'bad' Chechens who opposed it), the same subterfuge extended to talking to 'good' Chechen officials, whom of course I had known for a long time, and many of whom, before they were 'good' officials, had sheltered me in their homes in the most trying months of the war. Now we can meet only in secret because I am a pariah, an enemy. Indeed, an incorrigible enemy not amenable to re-education.

I'm not joking. Some time ago Vladislav Surkov, Deputy-Head of the Presidential Administration, explained that there were people who were enemies but whom you could talk sense into, and there were incorrigible enemies into whom you couldn't.

A few days ago, on 5 August 2006, I was standing in the middle of a crowd of women in the little central square of Kurchaloy, a dusty village in Chechnya. I was wearing a headscarf folded and tied in the manner favoured by many women of my age in Chechnya, not covering the head completely, but not leaving it uncovered either. This was essential if I was not to be identified, in which case nobody could say what might happen.

To one side of the crowd a man's tracksuit trousers were draped over the gas pipeline which runs the length of Kurchaloy. They were caked with blood. His severed head had been taken away by then and I didn't see it.

During the night of 27–8 July two Chechen fighters had been ambushed on the outskirts of Kurchaloy by units of the pro-Kremlin Ramzan Kadyrov. One, Adam Badaev, was captured and the other, Hoj-Ahmed Dushaev, a native of Kurchaloy, was killed. Towards dawn not far short of twenty Zhiguli cars, full of armed people, drove into the centre of the village and up to the district police station. They had Dushaev's head with them. Two of the men suspended it in the centre of the village from the pipeline, and beneath it they hung the bloodstained trousers I was now seeing.

The armed men spent the next two hours photographing the head with their mobile phones.

The head was left there for twenty-four hours, after which militiamen removed it but left the trousers where they were. Agents of the Procurator-General's Office began investigating the scene of the fighting, and local people heard one of the officers ask a subordinate, 'Have they finished sewing the head back on yet?'

The body of Dushaev, with its head now sewn back in place, was brought to the scene of the ambush and the Procurator-General's Office began examining the scene of the incident in accordance with normal investigative procedures.

I wrote about this in my newspaper, refraining from comment beyond dotting a few *i*'s in respect of what had happened.

I reached Chechnya at exactly the same time as the issue of our newspaper with the article. The women in the crowd tried to conceal me because they were sure the Kadyrov people would shoot me on the spot if they knew I was there. That reminded me that Kadyrov's government has publicly vowed to murder me. It was actually said at a meeting that his government had had enough, and I was a condemned woman. I was told about it by members of the government.

What for? For not writing the way Kadyrov wanted? 'Anybody who is not one of us is an enemy.' Surkov said so, and Surkov is Ramzan Kadyrov's main supporter in Putin's entourage.

'Ramzan told me, "She is so stupid she doesn't know the value of money. I offered her money but she didn't take it,"' an old acquaintance, a senior officer in militia special forces, told me that same day.

I met him secretly. He is 'one of us', unlike me, and would face difficulties if we were caught conferring. When it was time for me to leave it was already evening, and he urged me to stay in this secure location. He was afraid I would be killed. 'You mustn't go out,' he told me.

I decided to leave nevertheless. Someone else was waiting for me in Grozny and we needed to talk through the night, also in secret. My acquaintance offered to have me taken there in an OMON car, but that struck me as even more risky. I would be a target for the fighters.

'Do they at least have guns in the house you are going to?' he continued anxiously. The whole war I have been caught in the middle. When some are threatening to kill you, you are protected by their enemies, but tomorrow the threat will come from somebody else.

Why am I going on at such length about this conversation? Only in order to explain that people in Chechnya are afraid for me, and I find that very touching. They fear for me more than I fear for myself, and that is how I survive.

Why has Kadyrov's government vowed to kill me? I once interviewed him, and printed the interview just as he gave it, complete with the moronic stupidity and ignorance that are characteristic of him. Ramzan was sure I would completely rewrite the interview, and present him as intelligent and honourable. That is, after all, how the majority of journalists behave now, those who are 'on our side'.

'Why have you got such a bee in your bonnet about this severed head?' Vasilii Panchenkov asks me back in Moscow. He is the Director of the Press Office of the troops of the Ministry of the Interior, but a decent man. 'Have you nothing better to worry about?' I am asking him to comment on the events in Kurchaloy for our newspaper. 'Just forget it. Pretend it never happened. I'm asking you for your own good!'

But how can I forget it, when it did happen?

I loathe the Kremlin's line, elaborated by Surkov, dividing people into those who are 'on our side', 'not on our side', or even 'on the other side'. If a journalist is 'on our side' he or she will get awards, respect, perhaps be invited to become a deputy in the Duma.

If a journalist is 'not on our side', however, he or she will be deemed a supporter of the European democracies, of European values, and automatically become a pariah. That is the fate of all who oppose our 'sovereign democracy', our 'traditional Russian democracy'. (What on earth that is supposed to be, nobody knows; but they swear allegiance to it nevertheless: 'We are for sovereign democracy!')

I am not really a political animal. I have never joined any party and would consider it a mistake for a journalist, in Russia at least, to do so. I have never felt the urge to stand for the Duma, although there were years when I was invited to.

So what is the crime that has earned me this label of not being 'one of us'? I have merely reported what I have witnessed, no more than that. I have written and, less frequently, I have spoken. I am even reluctant to comment, because it reminds me too much of the imposed opinions of my Soviet childhood and youth. It seems to me our readers are capable of interpreting what they read for themselves. That is why my principal genre is reportage, sometimes, admittedly, with my own interjections. I am not an investigating magistrate but somebody who describes the life around us for those who cannot see it for themselves, because what is shown on television and written about in the overwhelming majority of newspapers is emasculated and doused with ideology. People know very little about life in other parts of their own country, and sometimes even in their own region.

The Kremlin responds by trying to block my access to information, its ideologists supposing that this is the best way to make my writing ineffectual. It is impossible, however, to stop someone fanatically dedicated to this profession of reporting the world around us. My life can be difficult, more often, humiliating. I am not, after all, that young at forty-seven to keep encountering rejection and having my own pariah status rubbed in my face, but I can live with it.

I will not go into the other joys of the path I have chosen, the poisoning, the arrests, the threats in letters and over the internet, the telephoned death threats, the weekly summonses to the Procurator-General's Office to sign statements about practically every article I write (the first question being 'How and where did you obtain this information?'). Of course I don't like the derisive articles about me which constantly appear in other newspapers and on internet sites which have long presented me as the madwoman of Moscow. I find it disgusting to live this way, I would like a bit more understanding.

The main thing, however, is to get on with my job, to describe the life I see, to receive every day, in our editorial office, visitors who have nowhere else to bring their troubles, because the Kremlin finds their stories off-message, so that the only place they can be aired is in our newspaper, *Novaya gazeta*.

Translated by Arch Tait

Orhan Pamuk

Orhan Pamuk, winner of the 2006 Nobel Prize for Literature, is Turkey's most celebrated author. His works have been published worldwide in over twenty languages.

Pamuk was brought before an Istanbul court on 16 December 2005, charged with 'insulting Turkishness' under Article 301 of the Turkish penal code. He faced up to three years in prison for an interview he gave the Swiss newspaper *Das Magazin* on 6 February 2005, in which he was quoted as saying that '30,000 Kurds and a million Armenians were killed in these lands and nobody but me dares to talk about it'. Pamuk was referring to the killing by Ottoman forces of thousands of Armenians in 1915–17. Turkey does not contest the deaths, but denies that its actions could be termed a 'genocide'. The '30,000' Kurdish deaths refers to those killed since 1984 in the conflict between Turkish forces and Kurdish separatists.

News of the interview for which Pamuk stood trial led to protests and copies of his books were burned. He also suffered death threats from extremists. The case against the writer, widely seen as a test of EU-hopeful Turkey's commitment to the democratic principle of free speech, was dropped in January 2006 on a technicality.

Pamuk delivered the following in New York on 25 April 2006 as the inaugural PEN Arthur Miller Freedom to Write Memorial Lecture.

In March 1985 Arthur Miller and Harold Pinter made a trip together to Istanbul. At the time, they were perhaps the two most important names in world theatre, but unfortunately, it was not a play or a literary event that brought them to Istanbul, but the ruthless limits being set on freedom of expression in Turkey at that time, and the many writers languishing in prison. In 1980 there was a coup in Turkey, and hundreds of thousands of people were thrown into prison, and as always it was writers who were persecuted most vigorously. Whenever I've looked through the newspaper archives and the almanacs of that time to remind myself what it was like in those days, I soon come across the image that defines that era for most of us: men sitting in a courtroom, flanked by gendarmes, their heads shaven, frowning as their case proceeds ... There were many writers among them, and Miller and Pinter had come to Istanbul to meet with them and their families, to offer them assistance, and to bring their plight to the attention of the world. Their trip had been arranged by PEN in conjunction with the Helsinki Watch Committee. I went to the airport to meet them, because a friend of mine and I were to be their guides.

I had been proposed for this job not because I had anything to do with politics in those days, but because I was a novelist who was fluent in English, and I'd happily accepted, not just because it was a way of helping writer friends in trouble, but because it meant spending a few days in the company of two great writers. Together we visited small and struggling publishing houses, cluttered newsrooms, and the dark and dusty headquarters of small magazines that were on the verge of shutting down; we went from house to house, and restaurant to restaurant, to meet with writers in trouble and their families. Until then I had stood on the margins of the political world, never entering unless coerced, but now, as I listened to suffocating tales of repression, cruelty, and outright evil, I felt drawn to this world through guilt – drawn to it, too, by feelings of solidarity, but at the same time I felt an equal and opposite desire to protect myself from all this, and to do nothing in life but write beautiful novels. As we took Miller and Pinter by taxi from appointment to appointment through the Istanbul traffic, I remember how we discussed the street vendors, the horse carts, the cinema posters, and the scarfless and scarf-wearing women that are always so interesting to Western observers. But I clearly remember one image: at one end of a very long corridor in the Istanbul Hilton, my friend and I are whispering to each other with some agitation, while at the other end, Miller and Pinter are whispering in the shadows with the same dark intensity. This image remained engraved in my troubled mind, I think, because it illustrated the great distance between our complicated histories and theirs, while suggesting at the same time that a consoling solidarity among writers was possible.

I felt the same sense of mutual pride and shared shame in every other meeting we attended – room after room of troubled and chain-smoking men. I knew this because sometimes it was expressed openly, and sometimes I felt it myself or sensed it in other people's gestures and expressions. The writers, thinkers, and journalists with whom we were meeting mostly defined themselves as leftists in those days, so it could be said that their troubles had much to do with the freedoms held dear by Western liberal democracies. Twenty years on, when I see that half of these people – or thereabouts, I don't have the precise numbers – now align themselves with a nationalism that is at odds with Westernization and democracy, I of course feel sad.

My experience as a guide, and other like experiences in later years, taught me something that we all know but that I would like to take this opportunity to emphasize. Whatever the country, freedom of thought and expression are universal human rights. These freedoms, which modern people long for as much as bread and water, should never be limited by using nationalist sentiment, moral sensitivities, or – worst of all – business or military interests. If many nations outside the West suffer poverty in shame, it is not because they have freedom of expression but because they don't. As for those who emigrate from these poor countries to the West or the North to escape economic hardship and brutal repression – as we know, they sometimes find themselves further brutalized by the racism they encounter in rich countries. Yes, we must also be alert to those who denigrate immigrants and minorities for their religion, their ethnic roots, or the oppression that the governments of the countries they've left behind have visited on their own people.

But to respect the humanity and religious beliefs of minorities is not to suggest that we should limit freedom of thought on their behalf. Respect for the rights of religious or ethnic minorities should never be an excuse to violate freedom of speech. We writers should never hesitate on this matter, no matter how 'provocative' the pretext. Some of us have a better understanding of the West, some of us have more affection for those who live in the East, and some, like me, try to keep our hearts open to both sides of this slightly artificial divide, but our natural attachments and our desire to understand those unlike us should never stand in the way of our respect for human rights.

I always have difficulty expressing my political judgements in a clear, emphatic, and strong way – I feel pretentious, as if I'm saying things that are not quite true. This is because I know I cannot reduce my thoughts about life to the music of a single voice and a single point of view – I am, after all, a novelist, the kind of novelist who makes it his business to identify with all of his characters, especially the bad ones. Living as I do in a world where, in a very short time, someone who has been a victim of tyranny and oppression can suddenly become one of the oppressors, I know also that holding strong beliefs about the nature of things and people is itself a difficult enterprise. I do also believe that most of us entertain these contradictory thoughts simultaneously, in a spirit of good will and with the best of intentions. The pleasure of writing novels comes from exploring this peculiarly modern condition whereby people are forever contradicting their own minds. It is because our modern minds are so slippery that freedom of expression becomes so important: we need it to understand ourselves, our shady, contradictory, inner thoughts, and the pride and shame that I mentioned earlier.

So let me tell another story that might cast some light on the shame and pride I felt twenty years ago while I was taking Miller and Pinter around Istanbul. In the ten years following their visit, a series of coincidences fed by good intentions, anger, guilt, and personal animosities led to my making a series of public statements on freedom of expression that bore no relation to my novels, and before long I had taken on a political persona far more powerful than I had ever intended. It was at about this time that the Indian author of a United Nations report on freedom of expression in my part of the world – an elderly gentleman – came to Istanbul and looked me up. As it happened, we, too, met at the Hilton Hotel. No sooner had we sat down at a table than the Indian gentleman asked me a question that still echoes strangely in my mind: 'Mr Pamuk, what is there going on in your country that you would like to explore in your novels but shy away from, due to legal prohibitions?'

There followed a long silence. Thrown by his question, I thought and thought and thought. I plunged into an anguished Dostoyevskyan self-interrogation. Clearly, what the gentleman from the UN wished to ask was, 'Given your country's taboos, legal prohibitions, and oppressive policies, what is going unsaid?' But because he had – out of a desire to be polite, perhaps? – asked the eager young writer sitting across from him to consider the question in terms of his own novels, I, in my inexperience, took his question literally. In the Turkey of ten years ago, there were many more subjects kept closed by laws and oppressive state policies than there are today, but as I went through them one by one, I could find none that I wished to explore 'in my novels'. But I knew, nonetheless, that if I said, 'There is nothing I wish to write in my novels that I am not able to discuss,' I'd be giving the wrong impression. For I'd already begun to speak often and openly about all these dangerous subjects outside my novels. Moreover, didn't I often and angrily fantasize about raising these subjects in my novels, just because they happened to be forbidden? As I thought all this through, I was at once ashamed of my silence, and reconfirmed in my belief that freedom of expression has its roots in pride, and is, in essence, an expression of human dignity.

I have personally known writers who have chosen to raise forbidden topics purely because they were forbidden. I think I am no different. Because when another writer in another house is not free, no writer is free. This, indeed, is the spirit that informs the solidarity felt by PEN, by writers all over the world.

Sometimes my friends rightly tell me or someone else, 'You shouldn't have put it quite like that; if only you had worded it like this, in a way that no one would find offensive, you wouldn't be in so much trouble now.' But to change one's words and package them in a way that will be acceptable to everyone in a repressed culture, and to become skilled in this arena, is a bit like smuggling forbidden goods through customs, and as such, it is shaming and degrading.

… I have related all these stories to illustrate a single truth – that the joy of freely saying whatever we want to say is inextricably linked with human dignity. So let us now ask ourselves how 'reasonable' it is to denigrate cultures and religions, or, more to the point, to mercilessly bomb countries, in the name of democracy and freedom of thought. My part of the world is not more democratic after all these killings. In the war against Iraq, the tyrannization and heartless murder of almost 100,000 people has brought neither peace nor democracy. To the contrary, it has served to ignite nationalist, anti-Western anger. Things have become a great deal more difficult for the small minority who are struggling for democracy and secularism in the Middle East. This savage, cruel war is the shame of America and the West. Organizations like PEN and writers like Harold Pinter and Arthur Miller are its pride.

Translated by Maureen Freely

Aung San Suu Kyi

The Nobel Prize-winner Aung San Suu Kyi is the leader of the National League for Democracy (NLD) in Burma and a writer. She has spent a large part of the last seventeen years in detention in Rangoon, much of it in solitary confinement. Suu Kyi was held under *de facto* house arrest for six years from July 1989 to July 1995, and again from September 2000 until May 2002, when she was released. Most recently, she was taken into 'protective custody' following violent clashes between opposition and pro-government supporters on 30 May 2003. As well as a number of fatalities, many people were injured, including Suu Kyi, who suffered cuts to the face and shoulder when the window of her car was shattered by a brick.

Suu Kyi is the author of many books, including *Freedom from Fear* (1991), *Letters from Burma* (1997) and *The Voice of Hope* (1997).

The following essay was first released for publication by Michael Aris, the editor of Freedom from Fear *and late husband of Suu Kyi, to commemorate the European Parliament awarding her the 1990 Sakharov Prize for Freedom of Thought. The award ceremony took place in Suu Kyi's absence at Strasbourg on 10 July 1991.*

Freedom from fear

It is not power that corrupts but fear. Fear of losing power corrupts those who wield it and fear of the scourge of power corrupts those who are subject to it. Most Burmese are familiar with the four *a-gati*, the four kinds of corruption. *Chanda-gati*, corruption induced by desire, is deviation from the right path in pursuit of bribes or for the sake of those one loves. *Dosa-gati* is taking the wrong path to spite those against whom one bears ill will, and *moga-gati* is aberration due to ignorance. But perhaps the worst of the four is *bhaya-gati*, for not only does *bhaya*, fear, stifle and slowly destroy all sense of right and wrong, it so often lies at the root of the other three kinds of corruption.

Just as *chanda-gati*, when not the result of sheer avarice, can be caused by fear of want or fear of losing the goodwill of those one loves, so fear of being surpassed, humiliated or injured in some way can provide the impetus for ill will. And it would be difficult to dispel ignorance unless there is freedom to pursue the truth unfettered by fear. With so close a relationship between fear and corruption it is little wonder that in any society where fear is rife corruption in all forms becomes deeply entrenched.

Public dissatisfaction with economic hardships has been seen as the chief cause of the movement for democracy in Burma, sparked off by the student demonstrations of 1988. It is true that years of incoherent policies, inept official measures, burgeoning inflation and falling real income had turned the country into an economic shambles. But it was more than the difficulties of eking out a barely acceptable standard of living that had eroded the patience of a traditionally good-natured, quiescent people – it was also the humiliation of a way of life disfigured by corruption and fear.

The students were protesting not just against the death of their comrades but against the denial of their right to life by a totalitarian regime which deprived the present of meaning-fulness and held out no hope for the future. And because the students' protests articulated the frustrations of the people at large, the demonstrations quickly grew into a nationwide movement. Some of its keenest supporters were businessmen who had developed the skills and the contacts necessary not only to survive but to prosper within the system. But their affluence offered them no genuine sense of security or fulfilment, and they could not but see that if they and their fellow citizens, regardless of economic status, were to achieve a worthwhile existence, an accountable administration was at least a necessary if not a sufficient condition. The people of Burma had wearied of a precarious state of passive apprehension where they were 'as water in the cupped hands' of the powers that be.

> Emerald cool we may be
> As water in cupped hands
> But oh that we might be
> As splinters of glass
> In cupped hands.

Glass splinters, the smallest with its sharp, glinting power to defend itself against hands that try to crush, could be seen as a vivid symbol of the spark of courage that is an essential attribute of those who would free themselves from the grip of oppression. Bogyoke Aung San regarded himself as a revolutionary and searched tirelessly for answers to the problems that beset Burma during her times of trial. He exhorted the people to develop courage: 'Don't just depend on the courage and intrepidity of others. Each and every one of you must make sacrifices to become a hero possessed of courage and intrepidity. Then only shall we all be able to enjoy true freedom.'

The effort necessary to remain uncorrupted in an environment where fear is an integral part of everyday existence is not immediately apparent to those fortunate enough to live in states governed by the rule of law. Just laws do not merely prevent corruption by meting out impartial punishment to offenders. They also help to create a society in which people can fulfil the basic requirements necessary for the preservation of human dignity without recourse to corrupt practices. Where there are no such laws, the burden of upholding the principles of justice and common decency falls on the ordinary people. It is the cumulative effect on their sustained effort and steady endurance which will change a nation where reason and conscience are warped by fear into one where legal rules exist to promote man's desire for harmony and justice while restraining the less desirable destructive traits in his nature.

In an age when immense technological advances have created lethal weapons which could be, and are, used by the powerful and the unprincipled to dominate the weak and the helpless, there is a compelling need for a closer relationship between politics and ethics at both the national and international levels. The Universal Declaration of Human Rights of the United Nations proclaims that 'every individual and every organ of society' should strive to promote the basic rights and freedoms to which all human beings regardless of race, nationality or religion are entitled. But as long as there are governments whose authority is founded on coercion rather than on the mandate of the people, and interest groups which place short-term profits above long-term peace and prosperity, concerted international action to protect and promote human rights will remain at best a partially realized struggle. There will continue to be arenas of struggle where victims of oppression have to draw on their own inner resources to defend their inalienable rights as members of the human family.

The quintessential revolution is that of the spirit, born of an intellectual conviction of the need for change in those mental attitudes and values which shape the course of a nation's development. A revolution which aims merely at changing official policies and institutions with a view to an improvement in material conditions has little chance of genuine success. Without a revolution of the spirit, the forces which produced the iniquities of the old order would continue to be operative, posing a constant threat to the process of reform and regeneration. It is not enough merely to call for freedom, democracy and human rights. There has to be a united determination to persevere in the struggle, to make sacrifices in the name of enduring truths, to resist the corrupting influences of desire, ill will, ignorance and fear.

Saints, it has been said, are the sinners who go on trying. So free men are the oppressed who go on trying and who in the process make themselves fit to bear the responsibilities and to uphold the disciplines which will maintain a free society. Among the basic freedoms to which men aspire that their lives might be full and uncramped, freedom from fear stands out as both a means and an end. A people who would build a nation in which strong, democratic institutions are firmly established as a guarantee against state-induced power must first learn to liberate their own minds from apathy and fear.

Always one to practise what he preached, Aung San himself constantly demonstrated courage – not just the physical sort but the kind that enabled him to speak the truth, to stand by his word, to accept criticism, to admit his faults, to correct his mistakes, to respect the opposition, to parley with the enemy and to let people be the judge of his worthiness as a leader. It is for such moral courage that he will always be loved and respected in Burma – not merely as a warrior hero but as the inspiration and conscience of the nation. The words used by Jawaharlal Nehru to describe Mahatma Gandhi could well be applied to Aung San: 'The essence of his teaching was fearlessness and truth, and action allied to these, always keeping the welfare of the masses in view.'

Gandhi, that great apostle of non-violence, and Aung San, the founder of a national army, were very different personalities, but as there is an inevitable sameness about the challenges of authoritarian rule anywhere at any time, so there is a similarity in the intrinsic qualities of those who rise up to meet the challenge. Nehru, who considered the instillation of courage in the people of India one of Gandhi's greatest achievements, was a political modernist, but as he assessed the needs for a twentieth-century movement for independence, he found himself looking back to the philosophy of ancient India: 'The greatest gift for an individual or a nation … was *abhaya*, fearlessness, not merely bodily courage but absence of fear from the mind.'

Fearlessness may be a gift but perhaps more precious is the courage acquired through endeavour, courage that comes from cultivating the habit of refusing to let fear dictate one's actions, courage that could be described as 'grace under pressure' – grace which is renewed repeatedly in the face of harsh, unremitting pressure.

Within a system which denies the existence of basic human rights, fear tends to be the order of the day. Fear of imprisonment, fear of torture, fear of death, fear of losing friends, family, property or means of livelihood, fear of poverty, fear of isolation, fear of failure. A most insidious form of fear is that which masquerades as common sense or even wisdom, condemning as foolish, reckless, insignificant or futile the small, daily acts of courage which help to preserve man's self-respect and inherent human dignity. It is not easy for a people conditioned by fear under the iron rule of the principle that might is right to free themselves from the enervating miasma of fear. Yet even under the most crushing state machinery courage rises up again and again, for fear is not the natural state of civilized man.

The wellspring of courage and endurance in the face of unbridled power is generally a firm belief in the sanctity of ethical principles combined with a historical sense that despite all setbacks the condition of man is set on an ultimate course for both spiritual and material advancement. It is his capacity for self-improvement and self-redemption which most distinguishes man from the mere brute. At the root of human responsibility is the concept of perfection, the urge to achieve it, the intelligence to find a path towards it, and the will to follow that path if not to the end at least the distance needed to rise above individual limitations and environmental impediments. It is man's vision of a world fit for rational, civilized humanity which leads him to dare and to suffer to build societies free from want and fear. Concepts such as truth, justice and compassion cannot be dismissed as trite when these are often the only bulwarks which stand against ruthless power.

Paul Kamara

The founding editor of the newspaper *For Di People*, Paul Kamara was sentenced on 5 October 2004 to two concurrent two-year prison sentences for an article highlighting a 1967 Commission of Inquiry into fraud allegations concerning the Sierra Leone Produce Marketing Board and the Ministry of Trade and Industry. President Kabbah had been a Permanent Secretary at the Ministry before taking presidential office and was then found guilty of fraudulent dealings by the Commission. The article claimed that the president should be barred from holding political office because those convicted of fraud are constitutionally barred from standing for election. Kamara was found guilty of 'seditious libel', by a judge whose impartiality has been called into question. He was released on 29 November 2005, when the Freetown appeal court overturned both convictions.

The following extract from a speech Paul Kamara gave in Italy in 2001, gives the background to the persecution he suffered in Sierra Leone prior to his most recent imprisonment.

I was born in Kambia district. My parents are from humble farming stock. Kambia district is one of the most neglected districts in what was, even then, one of the poorest countries in the world. Thanks to my parents and the Catholic Mission I was able to receive a decent education, but it was a struggle. I was more fortunate than most of my contemporaries, I must confess.

By the early 1970s, as I was struggling through school on a single meal a day, the ruling All Peoples Congress (APC) had turned itself into a corrupt *de facto* one-party dictatorship. It had eliminated formal opposition parties, and dissidents in its own ranks. Free speech was curtailed and a cult of the leader – rivalling anything promulgated in Stalinist Russia – was gradually growing up around then President, Siaka Stevens.

It was in this atmosphere that school friends and I joined the anti-All Peoples Congress demonstration of January 1977. These riots were sparked off when a peaceful demonstration caused a brutal reaction from the regime.

I entered Fourah Bay College in 1978 and because of my poor background and due to the fact that the APC, in order to tame students, had begun to slash university scholarships, life was really a struggle.

The one-party state was now officially declared, through a rigged referendum and the constitution of 1978.

For Di People newspaper was born in 1983, a year after I graduated from university. From day one, we tried to make our publication a real newspaper born out of a strong sense for humanity, freedom and justice.

Ironically, it was precisely these values that got me imprisoned in 1984, after less than four months acting as *For Di People*'s editor. We ran a story exposing how President Stevens had taken the Star of Sierra Leone – the third-largest diamond ever found – abroad for sale. This was how our country was run then. I recall *Time* (in one of the rare stories on the situation in Sierra Leone written by a Western magazine during those days) remarking drily that 'President Stevens often confused the treasury with his personal bank account'.

For my pains I was whisked off into solitary confinement and held in damp and unhealthy conditions for over ten days. No charges were ever brought against me. Everyone, including

Stevens, knew that the story was completely true. My crime in the eyes of the state was to tell truths which, in their opinion, should best be whispered.

A few months later I was back inside the dreaded Pademba Road maximum-security prison for a much longer spell, this time for exposing a deal involving an inflated contract for the purchase of uniforms for our military police.

I have been jailed more times than I can recount, and seen inmates die in droves, many because of a corrupt judicial system manipulated by a despotic regime. I wrote an article in which I compared that prison to a silencer that whispers a soft, painful, and agonizing death.

I shall not burden you with all the travails we went through during those bitter days; my illegal abduction and detention on a false bench warrant signed by a magistrate who had been bribed by a gang of crooked foreign contractors whom we'd exposed; the temporary 'banning' of our newspaper in 1988 – only reversed following a popular outcry – and our protracted battle with the Inspector-General of Police – the most powerful and feared man in the country – during the days of Siaka Stevens's successor, Major-General Joseph Saidu Momoh.

By this time the APC was universally detested for its corruption and incompetence. *For Di People* was no longer walking alone as it was. To broaden our base we set up the National League for Human Rights. By then the winds of political change were blowing; the same winds that toppled the Berlin Wall also shook the far less sturdy barriers of the one-party dictatorship. We were poised to play an active role in ensuring a level playing field for free, democratic elections when two disasters hit almost simultaneously – war and a coup, in 1991/92.

The 29 April 1992 coup by a group of young officers was popularly hailed as a 'revolution', but within a year they had shown a streak of brutality which surpassed even the rotten dictatorship they'd overthrown. Our paper was the first to detail some of these human rights abuses – including the rape of a senior hotel manageress, beatings of people who opposed the military's will and the bloody executions of twenty-six people who were accused of being involved in a coup plot; even though most of them were already in detention when this phantom coup was being plotted.

The military refused to issue our licence in January, 1993. For almost two years we languished, but the National League for Human Rights took up the slack. We were able to support the eight detained journalists held in late 1993 for exposing the case of Captain Strasser, then head of state, who disappeared with a 100-carat diamond.

Even though our paper was not circulating, the military still considered us a threat. Both my news editor, Sallieu Kamara, and I were hauled before the so-called military council and accused of being 'enemies of the state'. My accusers eventually backed down.

When we finally won back our licence in 1995 we hit the streets with a bang; doing exactly the same things for which we'd been banned more than two years earlier. We gave our full support to the independent elections commission and also fully covered and participated in the two consultative conferences that led to the fixing of a date for free elections in February 1996. We covered and supported women's, students' and civil society groups who agitated for those elections.

On 26 February 1996, after voting along with the rest of my staff, we were sitting in a bar having a beer and quietly hoping that we'd live to see what we'd agitated for for almost twenty years: democracy. Suddenly, a curfew was declared.

On my way home, I was ambushed in front of the press house. More than fifty bullets were fired into my vehicle. I staggered out and dropped on the ground. They fired another shot into my leg and thigh, then a passing vehicle scared them off, and I was taken to the hospital.

I won't bother you with the long and painful period of operation after operation to repair my shattered thigh. I spent long days with my leg in traction, and had a slow and painful process of physiotherapy.

We denounced the killers and mobilized the population into civil disobedience for the next nine months, until the junta was flushed out by the West African peacekeeping forces.

One fateful day they came and flung me from the second floor of our office building. Had it not been for an international outcry, and particularly the BBC, which alerted the world to my plight, I would be dead by now.

Editor's note: During Kamara's most recent stint in prison, his position at For Di People *was covered by thirty-four-year-old Harry Yansaneh. On 10 May 2005, Yansaneh was attacked by a gang reportedly acting on the orders of a member of parliament. The journalist died of kidney failure on 27 July as a result of injuries sustained during the assault.*

Jiang Qisheng

In 2000, the Pro-Democracy activist Jiang Qisheng was sentenced to four years in prison in China for writing and distributing an open letter to commemorate the tenth anniversary of the 4 June 1989 crackdown in Tiananmen Square (see also p.10).

The following is Jiang Qisheng's open letter, translated and published in English for the first time.

Light a myriad candles to collectively commemorate the brave spirits of 4 June
An open letter

Compatriots, Citizens,

Fully ten years ago, a great and startling, tragic movement exploded throughout this land of China. It was a movement of resistance against corruption and bureaucracy; it was a democratic movement of speaking the truth and struggling for rights; it was a patriotic movement calling for transformation and the renaissance of China. During those fifty or so days which will for ever be etched into the history books, millions upon millions of compatriots were awakened by the humanity and conscience displayed in the actions of simple and solemn citizens. They raised the image of the people of China to great new heights; they coalesced to form one of the brightest moments in China's history.

However, this movement which revealed the will of the

people was denounced by the muddled and confused political authorities, who called it 'chaos' and a 'counter-revolutionary riot'. Outrageously, they mobilized tanks and machine guns to conduct their bloody massacre, creating an injustice, a false justice and an evil justice of such size that China and the rest of the world were horrified. The 4 June Massacre is one of the most inhuman acts of the twentieth century; it is China's shame, and it is the world's shame.

In the ten years since the 4 June Massacre, corrupt officials have congratulated corrupted officials, and corruption in government has become ever more fierce; power and money go all the way to the top, while fairness and justice are on the verge of death.

In the ten years since the 4 June Massacre, the loss of state-owned assets has accelerated, state-owned natural resources have been disastrously plundered, the rich are incredibly richer and the poor are so much poorer, and popular discontent is once again seething towards a crisis.

In the ten years since the 4 June Massacre, the same prohibitions on speech, on publishing and on political parties remain, and speaking or publishing the truth or banding together with like-minded people are still sure to cause consternation.

In the ten years since the 4 June Massacre, the families of the people killed and the people who were injured are still suffering in pain; prisoners of conscience are still in prison; and unemployed workers, helpless city-dwellers, and impoverished peasants have grievances but nowhere to take them, they have truths they cannot speak, and they have tears they dare not shed.

All of this tells us: in the forgetting and dilution of the 4 June Massacre, and in the stubborn ignorance that the assessment of the 4 June Massacre 'has not changed and will not change', natural justice continues to be violated, and human justice continues to be trampled. Morality is perishing, society is deteriorating; the people struggle to survive, the people's rights are wronged; transformation is refused and renaissance is a distant hope.

Compatriots and Citizens, to ease our conscience, for our fundamental interests, for social justice and for the future of the motherland, we must oppose this forgetting and reject these false charges; we must take a stand on the strength of our spirit and use the opportunity of the ten-year anniversary of the 4 June Massacre, extend a people's memorial, a citizens' memorial, a memorial from the entire Chinese nation throughout this precious vast land of ours. The types of memorial can be many and varied so that everyone is able to perform their own: on the evenings of the 3 and 4 of June in each home, lights can be switched off for an hour and a candle can be lit to illuminate our memories and shine on our conscience. One simple candle does not amount to much, but a million candles will fire our wills and bind our hearts and souls. And it will be a silent mourning, a mourning for the sacrifices made ten years ago for freedom, dignity and happiness. And it will be a silent condemnation, a condemnation of the atrocity of might crushing human rights; and a condemnation of the perversion when 'stability' crushed justice. And it will be a silent expression, an expression of yearning in the pursuit of freedom, the promotion of justice, the protection of human rights and the demand for democracy.

Compatriots, Citizens, as the night of 3 June approaches, let us light a myriad candles to collectively commemorate the brave spirits of 4 June.

Appendix: Suggestions for marking the tenth anniversary of the 4 June Massacre

1. No entertainment
On 3 and 4 June, deliverately avoid recreational activities.

2. Mourning clothes
Wear mourning clothes on 3 and 4 June.

3. Make telephone calls
Starting at nine in the evening of 3 June, let the sound of a telephone's ring be a sound of mourning and a demand for the return of justice.

4. Send pager messages
Starting at nine on the evening of 3 June, send the three words 'in silent tribute' to all of the people you know with pagers.

5. Send e-mails
On 3 and 4 June, send each other commemorative e-mails.

6. Send letters
Starting from 15 April, send letters of condolence to the families of people who were killed and to the people who were injured at the 4 June Massacre, and send a letter of condemnation to the Prime Minister, Li Peng.

7. Light a candle
On 3 and 4 June, switch off the lights in your home and light a candle to the brave spirits of 4 June.

8. Walk in unison
On 3 and 4 June, gather together with like-minded people and deliberately step out together and walk en masse and in unison.

Some braver citizens may also want to consider calling the

hotlines of international media organizations, distributing and posting commemorative essays, holding video evenings in their homes, or even going out to participate in public candlelit vigils.

15 April 1999

Translated by Ben Carrdus

Ma Thida

Ma Thida (pen-name Sanchaung) a short-story writer, editor and doctor, was arrested in Burma on 7 August 1993, accused of contact with illegal organizations, endangering public peace and distributing banned literature to foreign opposition groups. She was sentenced to twenty years in prison on 15 October 1993 under the Emergency Powers Act. During her detention she suffered from digestive problems, tuberculosis and ovarian tumours. Ma Thida was elected an honorary member of various PEN centres, and was finally released on 11 February 1999 under an amnesty on humanitarian grounds.

Ma Thida was unable to publish the following semi-autobiographical short story in her own country. It describes her own attempts to get her stories published and her experience at the hands of editors too embarrassed to admit that they are afraid of accepting her manuscripts because they are political, and critical of the government.

A novel response

The weather was unusually hot. At that moment it could have been a road in a desert that he was setting off down. No trees. Nothing. And worse still, he had shaved his head only that morning and he had forgotten his umbrella. Beads of sweat gathered on his head and trickled down his body. It was his fate, though. His karma. This must have been what Buddha had meant when he preached the Eightfold Path, which could free human beings from the pain caused by their desires. Still, he told himself, so long as he could not escape Samsara, the cycle of rebirth, he would go on trying to make his name as a writer.

Before becoming a monk, he had been a novice, and before he became a novice, he had been a *kappiya* layman serving in the monastery. And before that, when he was a little boy, he had grown up in the monastery. So he had a thorough knowledge of Buddhist rites. Not for him any 'grade-skipping' or 'jump promotion'.

The same was true of his love of literature. He had always been a bookworm. As a young boy in the monastery he had worked his way through the sutras and he could recite any of them you cared to ask for off the top of his head. He had also lapped up Burmese and ethnic minority folk tales and legends and children's poetry, like a cat in cream. As a *kappiya* he continued to learn Buddhism and more of Buddha's teachings by heart and from there he had moved on to novels, thrillers and love stories, stories about true life and three-line poems. As a novice, he neglected his studies of higher Buddhist philosophy, learning little more than the names of the texts. Instead of taking his lower-level religious exams, he took to reading short stories and writing poems, which were published in the local magazine under a layman's pen-name.

He was successful as a novice, but only in the literary sphere. He finally reached the point where he had almost forgotten the sutras. But by then his poems were appearing simultaneously in two journals and a magazine.

That was when he decided to give up studying religion and stop bothering with exams. He continued to practise meditation but he set his mind on making a name as a great writer. He had a vision that one day he would be fêted by his readers and editors and by other writers in much the same way as a novice who had come top in a religious exam.

He wrote short stories by the light of a kerosene lamp. And he did well. Editors told him that his stories were popular with the readers and they wanted more of them. He was pleased that everyone, including the critics, commented on how well the author understood daily life, despite being a novice. Later, his editors even started coming to the monastery, making offerings of fruit juice on bended knee and giving him fees for his manuscripts. Novices who passed their religious exams might get their names once or twice in the magazines. But his layman's pen-name, followed by his monk's name in brackets, appeared in almost every magazine almost every month. He congratulated himself for having made the right decision.

Until recently, that is, when something happened which badly dented his self-confidence. Suddenly, his stories started getting rejected by the editors. The editors – the arrogant one, the dumb one, the unqualified one, the bumptious one, the loud-mouthed one, the clever one, the pathetic one and the stupid one – they all stopped visiting his monastery to offer him fruit juice and bid for his manuscripts. In one magazine he found an article about a novice who'd come top in an advanced religious examination. The magazine was plastered with this novice's picture. He, on the other hand, was like a heron fishing by an empty stream, scouring the magazines for a glimpse of his pen-name, but never finding one.

Nonetheless, he was determined not to lose heart. One day, he slipped the manuscripts of three recent short stories into his shoulder bag and set off for the publishing houses of downtown Rangoon. He decided he would go himself and ask the editors what was wrong with his stories. He wanted to become a respected writer and he was determined to do everything he could to achieve his ambition.

'... Do come in, *Sayadaw* [Reverend].'

The editor greeted him deferentially. Things couldn't be that bad after all.

'I just thought I'd drop by. You haven't been using my stories recently. I wondered why.'

The editor, who was pretty dumb anyway, became more tongue-tied.

'Uh, um ... uh ... well, you see, you see, it's the reader-ship. The readers liked those stories you wrote when you were younger, but ...'

'When I was younger?'

'Uh, that's right, when you were younger, when you were still a novice. Like that one, "Moonlit Night". Yes, like that.'

'"Moonlit Night"? But I wrote that over a year ago. Yes, I was about nineteen at the time, so I was still only a novice. I'm twenty now, and a fully fledged monk. Anyway, I've just finished another story. Can I show it to you?'

He took the manuscript out of his bag and handed it to the dumb editor, who quickly glanced through it, stopping here and there to read a few lines. Then he handed it back to the monk, saying, 'It's too obvious. Readers nowadays don't like stories like this.'

The monk remained silent. To argue would have been damaging to his self-respect. He took his leave and carried on to another magazine.

'Oh it's you is it, *Sayadaw*? Have you come to deliver a manuscript? Do you think you could hold on to it for a little while longer? You see, we only use layman's scripts for the time being, up until *Waso* [Lent]. We won't be able to use yours until after the beginning of *Waso*. So why don't you hang on to it for the time being?'

So that was that. Short and sweet. Being a monk seemed to

mean that he would have to keep both precepts and manuscripts. As he walked on to the next magazine, the scripts in his bags seemed to weigh a bit heavier.

It got worse when he reached the next magazine house because he could not find the people he usually dealt with, the clever editor and the arrogant one. Instead, a man whom he had not seen before muttered something inaudible about them being out or gone away or not having got there yet. Then the man asked if the monk had dropped by to discuss a ceremony to lay the foundations for a monastery or hoist an umbrella onto a pagoda. At that point he started wondering if he should give up and go home. But since he had come all this way without managing to get one manuscript accepted, he decided to make a last attempt to restore his self-confidence. He would go back to the editor who had given him short shrift and try and talk to him again.

It seemed to be going OK. The blunt-speaking editor sat down there and then and read his manuscript, page by page, sucking on a cheroot. The monk tried to read his face. He thought he could detect a glimmer of enthusiasm. Things seemed to be looking up. At least the editor was giving the story, which was called 'The Middle Way', a fair wind.

'*Sayadaw* … erm … Novice … err Monk … your story … Yes … Well, the problem is it's not very easy for most people to understand. There's too much religion in it, you see. But it's very good. I do like it. Really, I do … So …'

'You'll use it?'

'Uh … well … you see, the problem is this. It's too religious for our magazine. Look, here's my suggestion. Why don't you write another one for us and we'll publish it. But not about religion, OK? I've always liked your prose style. We'll definitely use your stories. But only if they don't mention religion.'

The monk reflected on the editor's words, which seemed to say that he, a monk, should not write about religion.

'I see. Well if that's the way it is, would you mind giving me back my story and I'll be getting going.'

'*Sayadaw*, honoured monk, sir, please don't be angry. *Sayadaw*, I am most humbly apologetic, really, how can I put it respectfully?'

The monk retrieved his manuscript. His self-respect was shattered, but nonetheless the editor continued to apologize to him with due deference and esteem, interspersed with quite substantial embarrassment.

'*Sayadaw*, I really am most terribly sorry ...'

Translated by Vicky Bowman

Hrant Dink

On 19 January 2007 the editor Hrant Dink, aged fifty-two, was assassinated outside the Istanbul offices of his Turkish-Armenian weekly newspaper Agos. He was a prominent advocate of mutual respect between Turkey's majority population and its Armenian minority, seeking to provide a voice to the Armenian community and create a dialogue between Turks and Armenians.

Dink was charged a number of times under the strict Turkish penal code for 'denigrating Turkey' and 'insulting Turkish identity'. More recently, in July 2006, Dink was handed a six-month suspended sentence for 'insulting Turkish identity' for an article on the Armenian diaspora. He has always maintained that his aim was to alleviate the tensions between Turkey and Armenia. A week later, a new case opened against Dink. Like Orhan Pamuk, he was due to stand trial under Article 301 of Turkey's penal code, for referring to the 1915 massacre of Armenians as a 'genocide' during an interview with Reuters. Dink was awaiting trial for these charges at the time of his death.

The journalist was revered by human rights activists for his stance against bigotry, but was considered a traitor by Turkish ultra-nationalists. Just before his assassination, Dink had complained of receiving death threats from nationalists, and had appealed to the Turkish authorities for these to be taken seriously.

A young man suspected of the murder was arrested the following day. There were huge demonstrations throughout

Turkey, and tens of thousands of mourners attended his funeral on 23 January.

The following is an edited version of a speech he gave to the International Publisher's Association/International PEN panel discussion on Freedom of Expression in Turkey held at the United Nations Commission on Human Rights in April 2004. This subject was one very close to his heart and undoubtedly led to his murder. He identifies various problems but his speech also carries a positive message.

The Turkish State's concept of minorities covers only the Non-Muslim communities as defined by the Lausanne Treaty. The number of these minorities is about 100,000 people and the Armenian community constitutes the largest group with a population of 60,000 thousand.

Individuals from a minority group do not face any obstacles concerning economic freedom, being equal before the law, and with regard to human rights. The exception is that minority members cannot be high ranking soldiers, state officers or bureaucrats. Concerning religious beliefs, they enjoy complete freedom. But the vital problem is that they do not have an educational institution in which to raise any clergy.

The inability of Minority Foundations to obtain real estate

Unfortunately, minorities do not enjoy the same freedom as others when it comes to their institutional rights. The main problem is that minority foundations are not able to obtain real estate. Until thirty years ago, they could acquire property, but later this was prohibited. Moreover, the real estate they possessed prior to this date was returned to the Treasury.

Due to the increased complaints about this injustice, a law was ratified by the National Assembly on August 2002 enabling Minority Foundations to obtain real estate. However, despite the new arrangement guaranteed by this law, Minority Foundations have still not been able to register the property, which they possess. While the law seems to bring new rights, it has not solved the problem of unjust confiscation. In the past thirty years, more than thirty properties belonging to Armenian Foundations have been taken from them by verdict of the Court. The title-deeds have been cancelled, ninety-five per cent of them have been transferred to the Treasury while others have been returned to their previous owners.

Until now, there has been no attempt to return property confiscated by the State. It is the duty of the Government to immediately return the real estate to the Minority Foundations and to reimburse the cost of those given to private individuals at today's value. It is impossible to claim that injustice has been removed without this happening.

An example of the problems in education

Armenian pupils who wish to go to Armenian schools have to prove at the beginning of every school year that their parents are Armenian. There remains a problem with the registration of children of 'mixed marriages' (mother Armenian, father Turkish or vice versa). Today registration at school is available only to children whose fathers are Armenian, but not to those whose mothers are Armenian. This unjust and sexist registration practice should be lifted.

History books on the curriculum

For a few years, Turkey has been making certain efforts within the framework of the 'Struggle Against Unfounded Armenian Claims' and against the discourse and studies presented by Armenians throughout the world about the alleged 'Armenian Genocide'. An important part of these efforts is devoted to the works studied in school. A new curriculum has been prepared focusing on the *unfoundedness* of Armenian claims, and the text books prepared around this issue will be read in our schools in the next school year.

Meanwhile, on 14 April, 2003 the Ministry of National Education sent a circular letter to all schools, including Armenian ones, demanding that they organise conferences and composition competitions dealing with the struggle against 'unfounded Armenian Genocide claims'. Human rights associations and the Bar of Diyarbakir have brought suits at the Supreme Council stating that this circular letter is contrary to international agreements and that it can lead to feelings of hostility among children. But the Ministry did not withdraw the letter.

This mentality is wrong. It leads generations to be raised as enemies by dictating to children one-sided information about a subject on which even the adults are not agreed. In fact, school should be the place where information is questioned, not dictated.

Moreover, Armenian history cannot be taught in Armenian Schools. It is a psychological torture to demand that young people, who are prevented from learning their own history of 3,000, have lessons denying their history and identity and to expect them to write humiliating sentences about the same.

The fact that the Armenian Genocide is still a taboo subject is proven by two recent examples:

1. The film-screening of *Ararat* was hindered due to the threats of ultranationalist groups (the Ministry had allowed the screening).

2. When the news broke in the Armenian paper, *Agos*, that Sabiha Gökcen, (the First World War female pilot in Turkey, known as the adopted daughter of Atatürk, the founder of the Turkish Republic), may be Armenian in origin, there was a huge reaction. These varied from those claiming that her being of Armenian origin is a blow against the unity and integrity of Turkey, to questions about what kind of plots were behind the publication of such news. Of course, there was also a democratic reaction that Gökcen might well have been Armenian.

Afterwards a backbiting campaign was launched against our newspaper *Agos*, and myself as editor- in-chief, by columnists of extreme nationalist newspapers. An extreme nationalist group mounted a demonstration in front of the newspaper's building, crying out discriminating slogans and threats.

These developments reveal once again how difficult it is to speak about the 'Armenian issue'. Turkey should be able to take this historical issue back to its original territory, and out of the loaded political arena. This can only be possible by providing a free atmosphere of speech and expression, where alternative theses to the official stance can also be discussed.

The problem for teachers of the Armenian language

Because there is no Armenian and Literature Department at Universities, Armenian language teachers cannot be trained at an academic level. A department should be founded as soon as possible either at the Literature Faculty of Istanbul University or at one of the private universities.

Conclusion

No striking improvement has been witnessed within the last year concerning the relations of Turkey with her minority groups. Despite the good will of political power and the fact that laws have been accepted at National Assembly, the bureaucracy in charge of putting these laws into practice holds a contrary attitude to the laws and is continuously creating difficulties.

At the root of these problems, lies a mentality, that regards Armenians not as principal citizens of this country, but as foreigners, as 'others', who pose a potential threat against the security of the country. If this mentality does not change, it is clear that no great improvement can be achieved through superficial arrangements.

On the other hand, the tendency of many Turkish intellectuals to learn about Armenian history, issues and culture, to discuss them and to see the Armenian community as a source of richness for the country, gives some hope for the future. Undoubtedly, a Turkey which values all its different aspects would have much to contribute to the European Union.

Hari Kunzru

Hari Kunzru was born in London in 1969. His first novel, *The Impressionist*, was published in April 2002 and was shortlisted for the Whitbread First Novel prize, the *Guardian* Fiction prize, the British Book Award, the Saroyan prize and the *LA Times* Award for First Fiction. It won the Betty Trask Prize, the Somerset Maugham Award, and the John Llewellyn Rhys Prize, which he declined, owing to the presence of the *Mail on Sunday* newspaper as sponsor. It was named one of (US) *Publishers Weekly*'s best novels of 2002 and one of the New York Public Library's 2002 Books to Remember. In 2003 he was named one of *Granta* magazine's Best of Young British novelists. His second novel, *Transmission*, was published in June 2004. A short-story collection, *Noise*, was published in 2005. Hari Kunzru is a Trustee of English PEN and is a member of the Writers in Prison committee. He sits on the editorial board of *Mute* magazine, and is a patron of the Refugee Council.

Hari Kunzru wrote the following essay exclusively for the anthology.

Host not found

Sometimes the 'Don't be evil' policy leads to many discussions about what exactly is evil. One thing we know is that people can make better decisions with better information. Google is a useful tool in people's lives. There are extreme cases, we're told, when Google has saved people's lives.

Sergey Brin, Google founder, interviewed in *Playboy*, September 2004

As the internet enters its second decade as a mass medium, it's worth looking back at one of the old saws that was bandied around in the covered-wagon days, when Californian sages made gnomic pronouncements about the future and the rest of the world repeated them at dinner parties. 'The Net treats censorship as damage and routes around it'. These are the words of John Gilmore,[1] radical libertarian, Sun Microsystems employee number five and *bona fide* West Coast guru-gazillionaire, and for much of the last ten years they've been repeated as part of the founding story of the internet, along with a gloss about the Net's inception as a military communications network designed to withstand partial destruction by nuclear attack.

In a technical sense, Gilmore (who was talking to a *Time* magazine journalist in 1993) has been proved right. The internet has provided an efficient conduit for people to share all manner of information other people don't want them to, whether those people are government whistleblowers, child pornographers, political dissidents, intellectual property pirates or terrorists. From the Drudge Report to beheading videos, censorship is being successfully circumvented around the globe. Looked on from the neutral standpoint adopted by network engineers, this is proof of a robust system. Ethical or political judgements about the content of the information flowing through the networks aren't relevant. It's all data. We should celebrate.

However, around the world, people have also discovered that despite the abstractions of network architecture and the

---

1 http://www.toad.com/gnu

nostrums of boosters who predicted a 'new economy' free of material constraints, the internet is also a physical thing, which has its existence on real telephone lines, ISP routers, undersea fibre optic lines and hard drives humming under tangible desks. And it's used by people sitting in real offices with real doors that can be broken down by all-too-real police if the information they're sharing contravenes local laws – and in some cases even if they don't, but some foreign power strong-arms their government, as happened in Sweden in May 2006, when US diplomats provoked a police raid on an ISP hosting a popular bit-torrent tracker called the Pirate Bay.[2] The internet's ability to route round censorship has the character of an ideal rather than a reality, a theoretical property.

No one understands this better than the Chinese journalist Shi Tao, who in April 2005 received a ten-year prison sentence for 'divulging state secrets abroad'. A translation of court proceedings showed that Yahoo! Holdings (Hong Kong), a subsidiary of the American search corporation, had given information to Chinese state investigators allowing them to link the journalist to repostings on foreign-based websites of an internal message the authorities sent to his newspaper regarding coverage of the fifteenth anniversary of the Tiananmen Square massacre.[3]

Yahoo!, Google and other internet giants have argued that cooperation with state censorship is the price of doing business in China. With the hypertrophy of the Chinese economy, the financial temptations have proved too great, even for a generation of dotcom companies built on the barefoot idealism of their young staff. Google's oft-quoted motto is 'Don't be evil', which might have sounded cool in a Stanford coffee bar, but has lately become something of an international sick joke.

2 thepiratebay.org
3 http://www.rsf.org/article.php3?id_article=14884

The Chinese government runs one of the most determined and best-resourced censorship operations in the world. In recent years, prison sentences have been handed down for activities such as downloading material from Falun Gong websites or 'endangering state security' by participating in pro-democracy discussion forums. This censorship effort relies partly on a large number of human monitors, and partly on technological means, often built and configured by suppliers outside China. For example, Skype, the internet telephone company recently bought by eBay, has admitted incorporating censorship functions into its Chinese-language chat client.[4]

Search technology (the current darling of the stock market) plays a major role in this. A research project by three universities, known as the OpenNet initiative,[5] routed search requests through Chinese computers using Google, Yahoo! and popular Chinese search engines like Baidu. They found that searches on many 'sensitive' words were summarily cut off. 'Freedom', 'Taiwan', 'Falun Gong' and various terms leading to material critical of the Communist Party were routinely unavailable.

Whether in China or Chicago, we're now living in a world where access to information is partly controlled by private corporations, whose wish to 'comply with local regulation' may involve many layers of hidden decision-making about what we can see, read and hear. Lack of transparency in the process by which search results are produced means that we don't tend to see messages saying 'You have been banned by the government from visiting this site' or 'Someone will sue us if we let you see this'. Instead we get 'host not found' or no error message at all, just a timed-out connection or a crash we might attribute to some other cause. This is invisible censorship, hard

---

4 http://www.hrw.org/reports/2006/china0806/index.htm
5 http://www.opennetinitiative.org/

to detect, hard to prove. In Uzbekistan, the government uses a technique called DNS hijacking to divert users from banned sites to so-called 'modified mirrors'[6], fake versions similar to the originals in most respects, but containing misinformation or black propaganda. Without some basic technical knowledge, the substitution is hard to spot. Dissidents like Shi Tao now face a matrix of government, technology and corporate power which represents a fundamental change in the way censorship is practised and experienced around the world.

Beyond vague notions of 'corporate social responsibility' it is clear that global information companies do not feel they have any obligation to be open or transparent, let alone to maintain any kind of public space for debate or dissent. Indeed, in a world where foundational technologies such as search algorithms are valuable intellectual property in themselves and messages travel through chains of privately owned systems operating under different national laws and IP regimes, it can be almost impossible to know whether information is being buried or blocked, let alone what, how and by whom. Even in markets with no overt state censorship, the threat of legal action may be enough to take controversial information offline, a tactic frequently employed by corporations against critics or whistleblowers. Payments are routinely made and taken for positioning in search rankings: money buys visibility, not accuracy or fairness. We appear to be moving towards a world with a privatized knowledge infrastructure, where indexing, storage and transmission are all performed by unaccountable entities engaged in what Human Rights Watch has aptly termed a 'race to the bottom'[7] for access to eyeballs and renminbi. What price market share in a world dancing to a Chinese economic

---

6 http://www.rsf.org/article.php3?id_article=10761
7 http://www.hrw.org/reports/2006/china0806/

tune? Whose organs get harvested? Whose liver will your board of directors eat? Nostalgia for disinterested notions of truth or intellectual independence will not suffice to preserve freedom of speech through the coming century. It will take concerted political action and a revitalization of the notion of an 'unowned' public sphere, something which will be fought tooth and nail by both state and corporate interests. We are already living through a period of enclosures, in which the knowledge commons are being rapidly fenced off.

Social panic about terrorism and paedophilia mean that there's strong public support in most Western democracies for mandatory state access to private communications. In the permanent state of pseudo-war under which we now live, interior ministers constantly remind us that civil liberties must be balanced against the exigencies of security. Technologies such as strong encryption and anonymous remailing must, they tell us, be kept out of the hands of the public. Employment of such technologies must constitute reasonable cause for surveillance. Encryption keys must be handed over on demand. Local internet service providers must be forced to surrender data when required, preferably through real-time automated 'black box' monitors, connected to their systems. Monitoring of voice and data traffic by the US (and perhaps, one day, by China) must be facilitated. The list goes on.[8] Unfortunately for us complacent beneficiaries of liberal democracy there is a paradox at work here. The technologies which provide anonymity to the paedophile and the terrorist are also those which protect the political dissident and the whistleblower. The encryption which impedes government surveillance of its citizens is also vital to the global banking system – an interesting area where corporate and state interests are in direct opposition.

---

8 http://www.privacyinternational.org/

For human rights campaigners it is time to move beyond the sphere of protest and lobbying into an active engagement with information technologies, putting anti-censorship tools into the hands of those who need them, providing services and support to dissidents rather than campaigning for their release after they have been imprisoned. Preservation of the global public sphere, individual civil liberties at home and the safety of dissidents in totalitarian regimes are now inextricably linked. It's not an easy knot to untangle, but we must try.

Ken Saro-Wiwa

Ken Saro-Wiwa was one of Nigeria's most beloved writers, and was executed by hanging in Nigeria on 10 November 1995 (see also p. 135)

The following are edited extracts from Ken Saro-Wiwa's letters.

From a letter to International PEN dated 3 September 1993 following his release from detention on 22 July 1993.

I am delighted that literature led me to the realization that I had a specific responsibility for the Ogoni people as a part of the human race and that, using my pen, I could contribute towards the amelioration of the fate of an unfortunate people. I am happy to be a part of an organization like PEN which can put its intellectual and moral resources at the service of an otherwise unknown people. I am now convinced, more than ever, that the path of literature is the assured way to human salvation and to civilization. I hail the power of the pen.

From a letter to International PEN, dated 19 October 1994, while in detention.

The danger to me remains. The legcuffs came off after 65 days but I'm still held incommunicado with three armed guards outside of my door 24 hours a day! Mercifully, they've not seized my pen or my brain, although I've been told that my faithful companion, my tobacco pipe, might be seized next. My transistor radio and a MOSOP[1] Tee shirt proclaiming 'Spirit of Ogoni, Say No!' went about six weeks ago but my creative sprit remains and I've not yet lost my great friend laughter ... I expect the worst but I'm hoping for the best.

From a letter to his son, dated 3 December 1994, smuggled out of prison.

Dear son, This is going to be a longish letter – an epistle sort of – written in a hurry because I live by the minute, unsure what my captors will do next. The intention is to destroy me. I am currently in what should be called a 'hothouse', a filthy rat- and cockroach-infested largish room where I'm held in solitary confinement. The last time I was here was in the early days of my arrest. Then I was in chains, but there were 34 other Ogoni young men. Most of those have now been freed or are in the hands of the police. I remain in Army hands, under constant surveillance, able to get out thrice a day to perform my ablutions. I was brought here on 25th November. Before then, from about the 29th May, I was in more 'comfortable' surroundings, in terms of physical comfort, but again I was alone, three armed guards outside of my door. Had I not been a writer and given to solitary life, it would have been hell. For the start, I had no books and borrowed a Bible from one of my guards – which I read from cover to cover ...

To cut a long story short, my attempt has been to stay psychologically superior to my captors. It has worked so far. I am in good spirits, remain quite convinced of my cause, have been

---

1 The Movement for the Survival of the Ogoni People.

buoyed by the unflagging spirit of the Ogoni people ... and the support of the family ... I don't know if I succeed in giving you a sense of a barbaric system sitting on top of a people, dehumanizing them, turning them into the lowest of beasts ... in spite of the struggles of the few, this situation will persist for the next hundred years if all the people have not been ground to dust by then. Terrible vision, isn't it?

From a letter to International PEN, dated 12 May 1995.

Whether I live or die is immaterial. It is enough to know that there are people who commit time, money and energy to fight this one evil among so many others predominating worldwide. If they do not succeed today, they will succeed tomorrow. We must keep on striving to make the world a better place for all of mankind. Each one contributing his bit, in his or her own way.

I salute you all.

Acknowledgements

The editors would like to thank everyone involved in the making of this anthology, and in particular: Sara Birch, Ruth Fainlight, Moris Farhi, Mandy Garner, Mai Ghoussoub, Anna Kushner, Jeffrey Lee, Cathy McCann, Richard McKane, Elizabeth Middleton, Carl Morten Iversen, Kjell Olaf Jensen, Jaime Ramirez-Garrido, Debjani Roy, Rachel Segonds, Larry Siems, Joan Smith, Jane Spender, Cecilie Torjussen, Dixe Wills, Sara Whyatt, Anna Wilson. And to all at Profile Books for their encouragement, clear editorial advice and patience. Thanks too to the Information Programme of the Open Society Institute for their support.

Permissions

Every effort has been made to trace the copyright holders of all works included in this anthology. Any omission is unintentional, and the publisher would be happy to make due acknowledgement in future editions. Grateful acknowledgement is made to the following:

Chris Abani: poems reprinted by permission of the author and Saqi Books; copyright © Chris Abani, 2001.

Ali al-Dumaini: extract from his memoirs, *Time for Prison, Times for Freedom,* published by permission of the author; copyright © Ali al-Dumaini, 2004; translation by Judy Cumberbatch.

Yury Bandazhevsky: extract from *The Philosophy of My Life* copyright © Yury Bandazhevsky, 2005; translated from the French by Carole Seymour-Jones.

Faraj Ahmad Bayrakdar: extracts from *Mirrors of Absence* by permission of the author; copyright © Faraj Ahmad Bayrakdar, 2007; translation by Sinan Antoon.

Reza Baraheni: 'A Minor Mistake in Evin Prison' published by permission of the author; edited by Lucy Popescu; copyright © Reza Baraheni, 2007.

Flora Brovina: poems translated from the collection of Brovina's poems *Nazovi Me Mojim Imenom* (*Call Me by My*

Name), published by FreeB92 Samizdat; copyright © Flora Brovina, 2000.

Angel Cuadra: poems published by permission of the author; copyright © Angel Cuadra, 2007; translation by Ruth Fainlight.

Hwang Dae-Kwon: letters edited by Lucy Popescu, letters copyright © Hwang Dae-Kwon, 2007.

Andrej Dynko: 'Sacrificial Therapy' reprinted by permission of the author; in an edited version by Lucy Popescu; copyright © Andrei Dynko, 2006; translation by Ales' Kudrycki.

Rakhim Esenov: extract from *Ventsenosny Skitalets* (*The Crowned Wanderer*), edited by Lucy Popescu; copyright © Rakhim Esenov, 2003; translation by Rachel Segonds.

Akbar Ganji: two articles from his book *Dungeon of Ghosts*, copyright © Akbar Ganji, 2000; translation by Nilou Mobasser.

Asiye Güzel: extract from *Asiye's Story* by permission of Saqi Books; copyright © Asiye Güzel, 2004; translation by Richard McKane.

Chenjerai Hove: *The Burdens of Creativity in Africa – Reflections* by permission of the author; in an edited version by Lucy Popescu; copyright © Chenjerai Hove, 2004.

Ali Reza Jabari: letter published by permission of the author; copyright © Ali Reza Jabari, 2007.

Liu Jinsheng: letter published by permission of the author; copyright © Liu Jingsheng, 2007.

Paul Kamara: published by permission of the author; edited by Lucy Popescu; copyright © Paul Kamara, 2007.

Harold Pinter: 'Death' reproduced by permission of the author and Faber and Faber Ltd; copyright © Harold Pinter, 1998.

Anna Politkovskaya: essay published by permission of the author; copyright © Anna Politkovskaya, 2006; translation by Arch Tait.

Jiang Qisheng: 'A True Story of April Fool's Day' and 'Light a Myriad Candles ... An Open Letter' published by permission of the author; copyright © Jiang Qisheng, 2007; translation by Ben Carrdus.

Mansur Rajih: poems published by permission of the author; copyright © Mansur Rajih, 2007; translation by Ren Powell and Mansur Rajih.

Yndamiro Restano: *Prison* copyright © Yndamiro Restano, 2007; translation by Mandy Garner; letter to PEN copyright © Yndamiro Restano, 2007; translation by Maria Delgado.

José Revueltas: letter to Arthur Miller, copyright © José Revueltas, 2007; translation by Amanda Hopkinson.

Raúl Rivero: 'Family Picture in Havana' first appeared on the website *Words Without Borders – The Online Magazine for International Literature*; copyright © Raúl Rivero, 2005; translation copyright © Diana Alvarez-Amell, 2005; published by permission of Words Without Borders [www.wordswithoutborders.org]. 'After You, God' from *Pruebas de contacto*, published by permission of the author, in an edited version by Lucy Popescu; copyright © Nueva Prensa Cubana, 2003; translation by Anna Kushner.

Faraj Sarkohi: extract from *We Make Death Easy* published by permission of the author; edited by Lucy Popescu; copyright © Faraj Sarkohi, 2007; translation by Nilou Mobasser.